SALVATION HEALTH & PROSPERITY

SALVATION HEALTH & PROSPERITY

Our Threefold Blessings in Christ

DR. PAUL YONGGI CHO

Creation House
Strang Communications Company
Altamonte Springs, Florida

Creation House
Strang Communications Company
190 N. Westmonte Drive
Altamonte Springs, FL 32714
(305) 869-5005

Unless otherwise identified, Scripture quotations are from the King James Version of the Bible.

Contents

Preface

The Word of God is steadfast forever, but the aspect of the Word that we emphasize can vary with the change of the times and the surroundings. The aspect of the gospel we stress at the present time, when the Republic of Korea is striving to join the ranks of the advanced countries of the world, cannot be the same as the emphasis of preceding generations when our country was under Japanese colonial rule for 36 years.

Now that the time has come for our nation to stand side by side with other countries in the ranks of developed nations and contribute to the making of history, Korean Christians should have an attitude which is more productive, creative, positive and active.

It is a special joy for me to present this book, entitled *Salvation, Health & Prosperity*, in response to the call of our times and our nation. The truths of these threefold blessings of Christ are the foundation stones which formed my faith. At the same time it has been the philosophical basis for my preaching of the gospel. It is my prayer that this book will be read widely and will be used as an instrument to lead as many people as possible to the brighter and more victorious path, full of life and happiness.

I give all the praise and glory to the God of the Trinity, who has blessed me to be able to present this book to you.

Paul Yonggi Cho, pastor
Yoido Full Gospel Church
Seoul, Korea
November 30, 1977

(This version was translated into English in 1986.)

Foreword

In introducing Cho's book to you, I am stirred in my soul to tell you, or remind you if you already know, that God is a good God and the devil is a bad devil.

God is totally good and the devil is totally evil. There is no evil in God and no good in the devil.

In addition, contrary to the false impression that "hell-fire and damnation" preaching causes people to repent, there is indisputable proof that the way to win souls is to preach God in His essential nature, and as the God who sends His Son "that they might have life and that they might have it more abundantly" (John 10:10).

Dr. Paul says emphatically that it is the goodness of God that leads people to repentance (Rom. 2:4).

Yet the Word of God is clear that there is a judgment day coming, a hell to shun and a heaven to gain. No genuine preaching of the Word of God can afford to fail in teaching people the dreadful penalty for sin and the result of dying as a sinner.

But Jesus Himself said, "For the Son of Man is not come down to destroy men's lives, but to save them" (Luke 9:56).

Hundreds of scriptures from Genesis to Revelation concern God's goodness in bringing a greater prosperity to His children spiritually, physically and financially. Along with those and the absolute promise of resurrection after death, Cho's emphasis on the little scripture 3 John 2 is of utmost importance to every human being: "Beloved, I wish above all things that thou mayest prosper and be in health, even as thy soul prospereth." This verse is particularly relevant to those of us who desperately need clear-cut words from God as to the good way He feels about us and the whole-person prosperity He desires (above all things) that we have *before we get to heaven.*

In 1947, when I was a young pastor and university student with a wife and two small children, struggling to make ends meet, and at the same time trying to obey God's call that I should take His healing power to my generation, I was torn apart by those in the church who didn't believe God is a good God but that He is solely a God of judgment.

I had read the New Testament through over 100 times and the entire Bible through dozens of times. I had practically memorized Matthew, Mark, Luke, John and Acts. These books contain the only original information about Jesus' life and ministry, about His first disciples and about the early Christians.

I was almost over the obstacles of launching into a worldwide healing ministry. I was full of the Word of God, full of the Holy Spirit and full of faith and compassion. But something was missing that seemed so small and inconsequential—I needed a word from God to open my understanding about the one thing I lacked.

One day I opened my Bible at random and it fell open to 3 John. My eyes fell on verse 2, which I did not remember ever reading before, and these words were the missing part—the master key for me.

My wife, Evelyn, and I read it over and over, crying and rejoicing, feeling a surge of God's presence that we needed in order to invade the earth with Jesus' power to win souls, heal the sick, cast out devils and show suffering people that God is a good God—and that He wants to prosper them in every area of their lives.

Little did I know that thousands of miles away in tiny Korea would be a young man, Paul Yonggi Cho, who was destined to touch all of Asia and the world with the most effective church growth ministry in history.

When my books and tapes fell into his hands in the late 1950s, the Korean war had left the people so poor they were pulling bark off trees and cooking it to keep from starving.

Paul Yonggi Cho got hold of the deliverance message of Jesus Christ: 3 John 2 in particular burned in his spirit to lift his people and himself out of spiritual, physical and financial poverty.

In Asia, the part of the world where it was hardest to take the gospel, young Paul Yonggi Cho, who later became Dr. Cho, has built the world's largest church of 500,000 members that will soon have 1,000,000 members.

I have never encountered such a praying church, a giving church, a witnessing church and a church with an Asia-wide and indeed a worldwide vision.

Cho has taught these people to practice seed faith, to believe God and to put Him first in their lives. God is now blessing and prospering them— the same people of whom most were poverty-stricken when they came under his ministry.

The single most important thing is that these Korean Christians of Cho's church are using their God-given prosperity to win their neighbors to the church and literally to "pray their way through" every hindering force of Satan.

The book you are about to read puts particular emphasis upon 3 John 2. By doing so, the author unveils the message of the whole Word of God—that God wants to prosper you in every area of your life so that you may be a blessing to others as never before.

I am honored to introduce Paul Yonggi Cho's book and to tell you that I love this man of God. His God-ordained and anointed ministry means much to me personally—and to millions around the world.

Sincerely,
Oral Roberts
September 1986

1

God Is a Good God

When I started my ministry at a tent church in Pulkwang-dong twenty years ago, I had such complicated feelings that I could hardly bear it. The people to whom I tried to preach the gospel were living in a spiritually barren state, facing a wall of despair, and were so destitute that they had difficulty finding enough to eat.

While preaching the Word to them and feeding them, I found myself involved in gross self-contradiction, for the God I had learned about at the seminary seemed to be merely the God of the future. I could not find the God of the present to show Him to people who were living in such desolation and poverty. Where was the God of the present in Korea? This question stirred in my heart. Introducing the God of the past could hardly make any impression on those people; on the other hand, the urgent situation of their present state kept the Christ of the future from being preached to them. So I cried out to God. I cried out not only for them, but I cried out for myself: "Oh, my Lord! Where is the God of the present? With what can I give hope and new life to these people who are in despair, starved and poorly clothed? Oh, Lord! Where are You at this hour—You who are God to them as well as to me?"

I cried and prayed with tears day in and day out, earnestly seeking. After I spent much time in supplication, God finally spoke to my heart. His words, warm and full of hope, were a revelation to me. The word from God contained the truth of the threefold blessings of salvation, health and prosperity written in 3 John 2: "Beloved, I wish above all things

11

that thou mayest prosper and be in health, even as thy soul prospereth."

Since that time this truth has been the foundation of all my sermons, and I have laid the foundation of my ministry on this scripture. When I interpreted all Scripture in light of the truth of this particular portion, God began to manifest Himself not only as the God of the past and the future, but as the God of the present—who lives in present time. Furthermore, because of the power of this message, our church has grown into an international church and will continue to grow in the future.

Actually, people all over the world today are faced with many problems caused by a sense of nothingness, poverty and curse, and their cries ring out constantly because of their fear of disease and death. These people need the threefold blessings of Christ. During thirty trips abroad to the United States, England, West Germany, France and the Scandinavian countries, I saw clearly that people everywhere were in a situation which called for a revelation of these blessings. When this message was preached, many wonderful changes took place and the fire of revival began to burn.

When we understand the threefold blessings fully, we can interpret Scripture from Genesis to Revelation on the basis of the passages that speak of these truths. After that the truth in the Bible revives and shines in the light of new life, and that truth becomes clearer to us. Like blind men touching an elephant to comprehend its shape, those of us who read the Bible without this foundation cannot understand or interpret fully what we read. But when we read the Bible armed with this strong theological foundation, all Scripture is connected and the work of the living God is manifested clearly.

Before discussing salvation, health and prosperity, I would like to show you the entrance hall to the house of threefold blessings. This entrance hall is labeled "Our Good God."

Our Good God

The first person we must meet is our good God. Today people are not convinced God is good. They see God as a supernatural being who fills them with fear, who threatens them and takes away their happiness. Or they see Him as a God who does not want to have anything to do with them.

I was leading a crusade in Hamburg, West Germany, when a middle-aged woman came from Essen to see me for counseling. She was born and brought up an orphan in unhappy circumstances and was personally acquainted with sorrow. She had married a Japanese doctor who was a naturalized German citizen. Her husband loved her very much. She had three children and lacked nothing to make her life full and complete. She was well-to-do and lived in a good house, and her children were healthy. In a word, her family seemed to be happy. But fear was rooted in her heart. She was afraid that at any time God might take from her all those things that made her happy. She thought, I must suffer to make my faith true, but since I am so happy, God may at any moment come down and take away my husband and children or cause an economic problem for my family in order to test my faith.

She became restless because of her fear. Her husband, though a psychiatrist, could not help set her free from this fear by psychoanalysis, so she came to me for help. She added this to what I have already related: "Pastor, before long the misfortune will spread over me like a black cloud. I was born an orphan and suffered all kinds of hardships. Life is wonderful now, but how can I dare to enjoy the happiness I know? Pastor, what shall I do?"

"Sister, you are making a grave mistake," I answered. "God is good. The devil comes to steal, kill and destroy; but Jesus, the Son of God, came that we might have life and that we might have it more abundantly."

"Pastor, I cannot bring myself to believe that," she replied.

I began to share with the woman why God is a good God. I told her to open the Bible. "In Genesis, we see how God created the heavens and the earth and all things. Every created thing shows the character of its maker. On the first day of creation, He made light. Was it good when God saw it?"

"God saw that it was good."

"How was it when God made the firmament on the second day?"

"There is no mention that it was good."

"Because the firmament was the place where the devil would take the power of the air and take possession after the fall, God did not mention that it was good. Only in that place were good works omitted. On the third day, when dry land was created, isn't it written that God saw that it was good?"

"Yes, it is."

God saw that it was good on the fourth and fifth days also, and on the sixth day, when God made the beasts and man, He saw that it was very good. If God had not been a good God, He couldn't have made anything that was very good. I told the woman: "From the beginning God made only those things which were good. We know a tree by its fruit. Since everything God created was good 'fruit,' shouldn't we infer that the tree—or God—has to be good also?''

The woman shook her head and would not believe this. "Sister, listen!" I continued. "Has anyone ever seen God?''

"No.''

"Who saw Him?''

"Only Jesus saw Him.''

"Yes! He has seen God. Those things which Jesus said and did were all the things which God said and did through Him. Well, then, let's look into the life of Jesus. Did Jesus do good or evil? He did good works; He cast out unclean spirits; He gave peace to those who trembled from unrest and fear; He raised the dead. Can you find anything wrong in the works which Jesus did? Even His enemies admitted that He saved others when they nailed Him to the cross.

"Since Jesus did so many good things, how could the God who works through Jesus be a bad God? Jesus said, 'What man is there of you, whom if his son ask bread, will he give him a stone? Or if he ask a fish, will he give him a serpent? If ye then, being evil, know how to give good gifts unto your children, how much more shall your Father which is in heaven give good things to them that ask him?' (Matt. 7:9-11).

"Sister, listen! Didn't Jesus say here plainly, 'Your Father which is in heaven gives good things'? Take a look at the universe. How do you see everything? Is it in good order and beautiful? Open the Bible to Revelation 21. Are the new heaven and the new earth, that God is going to make, good or not? The Scripture says: 'Behold, the tabernacle of God is with men, and he will dwell with them, and they shall be his people, and God himself shall be with them, and be their God. And God shall wipe away all tears from their eyes; and there shall be no more death, neither sorrow, nor crying, neither shall there be any more pain: for the former things are passed away' (Rev. 21:3-4).

"It is written that God will not only thus renew our surroundings, but our weak body will be replaced with a strong body, the carnal with immortal. How can you refuse to believe that God, who only produces good fruit, is a good God?''

Only after that the woman nodded her head. "Hearing what you say, Pastor, I see now that God is a good God.''

"It is the devil who whispers to you that God may take away your happiness,'' I counseled her.

The devil planted fear in the heart of Job in the Old Testament. Job fell into such a tragic state because he harbored fear and dread in his heart. "For the thing which I greatly feared is come upon me, and that which I was afraid of is come unto me" (Job 3:25). Because of his fear, Job lost all he possessed: ten children, seven hundred sheep, three thousand camels, five hundred yoke of oxen, five hundred female donkeys, and male and female servants.

The devil whispered in the mind of Job, "God is not a good God. He will soon take away your children from you and kill both you and your family." As soon as Job was deceived by the devil's voice and lost the image of a good God, he trembled with fear. The devil accused him in the presence of God of this fear, causing Job to suffer severe punishment. The Bible says clearly, "There is no fear in love; but perfect love casteth out fear: because fear hath torment" (1 John 4:18).

When Job regained his faith, confessing that he would keep his faith even though God destroyed him, God gave him twice as much wealth as he had before.

Faith is like a gear in a car. When the car is in forward gear, the car moves forward. But when the car is in reverse, it moves backward with the same power. Likewise, if you believe that God is a good God, success will come to you; if you do not believe that God is a good God, you will encounter fear, unrest and despair. Your faith can be positive or negative. It is up to you. Positive faith produces positive faith, and negative faith produces negative faith.

At the entrance hall, before you enter the threefold blessings, you must put off all of your negative faith and believe firmly that God, who sent Jesus to be crucified for you, is good. As it is written, "He that spared not his own Son, but delivered him up for us all, how shall he not with him also freely give us all things?" (Rom. 8:32).

This God who loves us with His great breadth and depth of love is really a good God.

Whenever we say God is good, the devil feels pain, but glory is given to God. Today, in so many pulpits, God is misrepresented. Some ministers only present Him as a God who is waiting for sinners to make a mistake so He can judge them with stern and fearful punishment. The most tragic Christian is the one who has no hope. People who have this belief are like the elder son who appears in the parable of the prodigal son, whose image of God was that God never gave him a young goat so that he could enjoy life (Luke 15:29).

It is written in the Bible, "According to your faith be it unto you" (Matt. 9:29).

God who is good and rich will not come to those who have no faith in His goodness. Though the prodigal son went far away from his father and wasted his substance with riotous living, he came back to his father in faith, believing that his father would welcome him. His father put the best robe on him, put a ring on his hand and shoes on his feet and gave him joy and satisfaction by ordering the fatted calf to be killed in his honor.

The two sons had the same father, but one son did not even receive a young goat, while the other son possessed all the riches of the father. What made these two sons so different? They each saw their father with different eyes and different expectations.

Those who believe God is a good God come to possess a positive mind. As it is written, "All things work together for good to them that love God, to them who are the called according to his purpose" (Rom. 8:28).

Since they believe in a good God, good things are good per se. Even though sometimes they encounter things which are not agreeable, they can accept them because they know God will bring good out of them also. Therefore their faith is kept positive at all times.

The Cross and the Salvation of Jesus Christ

After filling our minds with the image of a good God, the next step is to change our misconception about the grace of salvation through the cross of Jesus Christ.

Thus far we have understood salvation only in spiritual terms. Our thinking has been of the conventional kind that the soul is saved and enters heaven when we leave this world. But the salvation which comes to us through the crucifixion and death of our Lord Jesus Christ and His resurrection from the dead is far deeper and wider than that. By His death on the cross and His resurrection, Jesus delivered us from the original sin caused by disobedience and the fall of Adam. Yet the fall of Adam did not end merely in the spiritual fall. The curse and death were the natural events which followed his spiritual death. He fell under that curse which drove him away from the garden of blessing. Physically, his body became the companion of death.

Therefore the salvation of Jesus Christ, which delivered us from the fall and the sin of Adam, is salvation in a wider sense. It not only changed our souls, but it changed our way of living from being a curse to being a blessing. This salvation also changed our flesh from being subject to death and disease to being subject to life. This is the message of the threefold blessings.

To understand more fully the salvation of Jesus Christ, we need to consider the exodus in the Old Testament, since it was a foreshadowing of the redeeming work of Jesus Christ.

One evening in the land of Goshen in Egypt, something very climactic took place. All at once the bleating of lambs was heard from every Hebrew house. A lamb was killed in every home, and the head of every household dipped some hyssop in the lamb's blood which had been kept in a bowl. Then they stroked the blood on the lintel and posts of the door of their home.

The heads of all households in the land of Goshen were hurrying to do the same thing. When it grew dusk outside, each family prepared for a long journey. They roasted the lamb they had killed, being careful not to break any of the bones, and they ate the lamb together with bitter herbs and bread that had been prepared without any yeast in it.

That night, at midnight, a great cry shocked the land of Egypt. The destroying angel of God passed through the land, entering every house which did not have the blood on the lintels and doorposts, and killed all the firstborn in the land of Egypt, "...from the firstborn of Pharaoh that sitteth upon his throne, even unto the firstborn of the maidservant that is behind the mill; and all the firstborn of beasts" (Ex. 11:5).

So the children of Israel arose, like a swarm of locusts, to leave the land of Egypt where they had lived as strangers for more than 430 years, and started on their journey toward the land of Canaan which God had given to their forefather Abraham.

The lamb which the children of Israel killed at that time was the Passover lamb. Jesus Christ became our Passover lamb. As the destroying angel *passed over* the homes where there was blood on the door, so today as many as depend upon the blood of Jesus Christ and come to Him are protected from the temptations and accusations of Satan and are exempt from judgment. When we read and "eat" the Word of God, the body of Jesus Christ, as the children of Israel ate the flesh of the lamb, we obtain strength and wisdom to overcome the world and win the victory.

God, who delivered the children of Israel by the blood of the Passover lamb, also led them by a pillar of cloud and a pillar of fire. By day, when it was hot in the scorching sun, God led them by a pillar of cloud to give them shade, and by night when it was dark He led them with a pillar of fire to give them light.

God divided the Red Sea and let them pass through it in the desert. He broke the rock to give them fresh water. In the wilderness He gave them manna and quail to eat. God became the Lord of hosts when they encountered the enemy. So God, neither slumbering nor sleeping, kept Israel until they passed over the Jordan River and entered Canaan, the land of promise.

In this record of their exodus, we find the broader and deeper meaning of the salvation which Jesus Christ gave us. Canaan, the land of promise, signifies the kingdom of heaven to Christians today. Until we Christians enter the kingdom that God has prepared for us, we will not receive the salvation which causes us to prosper in all things and be in good health. We are His children. Therefore our Lord says to us, "Beloved!" We are His, and He loves us so much He allowed His body to be nailed to that cruel cross. The "good God," who allowed the crucifixion of His only begotten Son because He knew this was the only way to redeem us, now wishes that we may prosper and be in health even as our souls prosper.

I assume that by now you have established a clear image of the good God in your minds and will come out of bigotry and prejudice to the salvation of Jesus Christ. It is time now to open the door to the entrance hall and enter the house of the threefold blessings. Lift up your eyes and look! There in front of us is the first room, and above the door is written: "As Your Soul Prospers." This is the room of the first blessing. Let's open the door and enter together.

2

As Your Soul Prospers

Why do you suppose our Lord said, "As your soul prospereth"? This passage of Scripture seems to indicate that at some time in the past something was wrong with our souls. What was wrong and how did it happen? What is the prosperity of the soul? What is the result of our soul not prospering? What can we do so that our soul can prosper now? We will find the answers to these questions in this chapter.

Man Is a Creature of Spirit, Soul and Body

"And the Lord God formed man of the dust of the ground, and breathed into his nostrils the breath of life; and man became a living soul" (Gen. 2:7).

"And God said, Let us make man in our image, after our likeness: and let them have dominion over the fish of the sea, and over the fowl of the air, and over the cattle, and over all the earth, and over every creeping thing that creepeth upon the earth. So God created man in his own image, in the image of God created he him; male and female created he them" (Gen. 1:26-27).

When God created the heavens and the earth and all things in them, God created everything by His word except man. He formed man of the dust of the ground with His own hands in His own image, and like Himself, and then He gave man the breath of life by breathing into his nostrils. The Hebrew word for the breath that God breathed into man is *ruak*, which means wind or spirit. When God breathed the breath of

19

life into man, he became a living soul. *Nephesh* is the Hebrew word for soul. Thus, when God breathed into the man that had been formed of the dust of the ground, his soul came into being.

As God Himself is the Trinity of the Father, the Son and the Holy Spirit, so we who are created in His likeness also have three parts: spirit, soul and body. "And the very God of peace sanctify you wholly; and I pray God your whole spirit and soul and body be preserved blameless unto the coming of our Lord Jesus Christ" (1 Thess. 5:23). Also, the human spirit, soul and body created in the image of God have the following different functions.

First, the spirit is the vessel which has God in it. Therefore, except through the spirit, we cannot know God. Through our spirit we praise God, pray to Him, worship Him and can know His will. People who are ignorant of God say there is no God because their spirit is dead. Moreover the spirit contains the conscience, which shows the right way of life. The conscience has the intuitive ability to know the truth of God. Therefore our spirit becomes the only way through which we can communicate with God.

Second, the human personality resides in the soul. Personality is the combined quality of knowledge, emotion and will through which man gets wisdom and thoughts, perceives the different feelings of joy, anger, sorrow or pleasure and makes decisions. Self-consciousness exists in the soul; so the soul actually is the personality. That is why the Bible calls the human being a soul.

Third, the body has five senses, namely, the ability to see, hear, smell, taste and feel. The spirit always recognizes the world through the body. Therefore the scripture, "as your soul prospers," means that the way leading to the prosperity of the soul is the balanced state of three parts in which spirit, soul and body function properly. This balance means that the spirit, according to the will of God, has dominion over the soul, and the soul has dominion over the body. The body gives up all of the lust of the flesh and obediently does what it is told to do by the spirit and the soul.

We can find such a creative balance of our threefold nature in Adam. Since Adam had God in his spirit before he fell, he communicated with God, heard the voice of God, lived according to the direction of a clear conscience and enjoyed the abundant blessings of God. Since his soul was ruled by his spirit, obeying the will of God, his mind was full of the knowledge of God and his emotions abounded in feelings imparted by the Holy Spirit. Because his decisions were made according to the will of God, he made no mistakes. Because his body was ruled by his spirit, and his spirit was full of the knowledge of God, he could temper his desires and avoid falling prey to excessive lusts. Adam was the man who lived spiritually and communicated constantly with God. He knew where he came from, where he was going and why he was alive. His five senses told him that his world was beautiful and perfect and that God was a good God. God the Father was the personal creator-God who wanted to communicate and have sweet fellowship with human beings. Man was made to serve God, to live spiritually according to the direction of God's Spirit.

Man, who was created with spirit, soul and body, had the function of a *vessel*. "What if God, willing to show his wrath, and to make his power known, endured with much longsuffering the vessels of wrath fitted to destruction: and that he might make known the riches of his glory on the vessels of mercy, which he had afore prepared unto glory, even us, whom he hath called, not of the Jews only, but also of the Gentiles?" (Rom. 9:22-24).

A vessel in itself has little value. Only when a vessel contains something does it have real value. Since we are made as vessels, we cannot know our value in ourselves; only when we have God in us are we of any value.

Vessels are inevitably filled with something. Unless we keep a vessel clean and fill it with some tasty food or use it for storage, it will be full of dust, so it will not long be empty. Human beings are receptive, and we possess either the Holy Spirit of God or the spirit of evil within our souls.

Some people say, "I have neither the Holy Spirit nor the evil spirit: I am neutral." This saying reveals ignorance. Man cannot help having either the Holy Spirit or the evil spirit within himself. When the Holy Spirit resides in our earthen vessels, our lives shine with vitality and we are honorable: "But we have this treasure in earthen vessels, that the excellency of the power may be of God, and not of us" (2 Cor. 4:7).

Man was created to be the temple of God: "Know ye not that ye are the temple of God, and that the Spirit of God dwelleth in you?" (1 Cor. 3:16). Since man was created to be the temple of God, he should have God within and live to worship God. Unless God lives in the human temple, an evil spirit will enter the temple immediately and make a dwelling place.

Man was made to have a spirit, soul and body, and was ordained to live with God in his spirit, in obedience to the will of God. Unfortunately, man broke the order of creation and sank into sin.

The Existence of Fallen Man

The word "Eden" means joy, and actually the garden of Eden was the garden of joy where all the necessities for Adam and Eve were beautifully prepared. God told Adam that he might eat everything in the garden except the fruit of the tree of knowledge: "But of the tree of the knowledge of good and evil, thou shalt not eat of it: for in the day that thou eatest thereof thou shalt surely die" (Gen. 2:17).

By the deceit of Satan Adam allowed Eve to persuade him to eat the fruit of the tree of knowledge, and man was sentenced to death by God. Dying is different from disappearing. Nothing disappears in this world. If a piece of paper is burned in the fire, according to the law of the constancy of mass, it turns into the same mass of gas and ashes. The paper is not brought to nothingness in the universe.

Man is like the paper. If a man dies, only the dialogue ceases between him and other people. The man does not disappear. When a man dies, the body remains, but it is unable to have dialogue with others and express feelings of joy or anger. Death means the severance of dialogue. As soon as Adam fell, his spirit was dead to God. As soon as Adam's spirit died, the dialogue between Adam and God stopped.

Some people ask: "Adam certainly ate of the fruit of the tree of knowledge, but he still lived, didn't he?" However, it was not the body of Adam which died, nor was it the soul of Adam which died. It was his spirit which died as soon as he committed sin.

As soon as the spirit of Adam died, God no longer dwelt in man. Since that time man has been cut off from God and cannot receive knowledge from God. Communication with God was severed. Man no longer knew where he came from or where he was going, why he was living or how he should live. From the moment that Adam's spirit died, those of his descendants who do not believe in Jesus Christ have no dialogue with God, for their spirits are dead. They cannot feel the grace of God in their hearts, though they can hear the word of God. They cannot be moved in their hearts by the Holy Spirit, nor can they understand the love of the cross until they repent. They cannot even feel shame or fear when they think of the wrath of God. Consequently there is no repentance.

After the fall, not only was the spirit of Adam dead, but he was also driven out of the garden of Eden. "Therefore the Lord God sent him forth from the garden of Eden, to till the ground from whence he was taken'' (Gen. 3:23).

Today, people who do not believe in Jesus Christ are driven out from God's presence. They are driven out of the bosom of God and the world of blessings. While they live in this world they wander like lost souls, not knowing their destiny or the direction in which they should go. Even though they have plenty to eat and expensive clothes to wear, live in fine houses and lack nothing, their physical surroundings vanish like vapor, and all that is left for them is endless wandering.

No one is more tragic than an outcast. An outcast can live for a time, but his end is like a leaf blown away by the wind. Nor did the fall of Adam end simply in the death of his spirit or his banishment from the garden of Eden. Because Adam and Eve were made in the image of God, they should have become obedient servants of God. Yet Adam and Eve refused to obey the Word of God and were deceived by the devil, so they became the servants of the devil. The Holy Spirit left man, who was created to be a vessel, and an evil spirit replaced the Holy Spirit. First John 3:8 reads, "He that committeth sin is of the devil; for the devil sinneth from the beginning."

Therefore, from that moment Adam and Eve belonged to the devil after they committed sin; they became his servants. In the vessel where God had made His abode, the devil entered and began his work. The work of God is to give life to His sheep and to give it more abundantly, but the work of the devil is to steal, kill and destroy. Adam and Eve were driven out of the garden of Eden where the tree of life stood, into the world of thorns and the briers of trouble, into hardship and despair.

If a person becomes the servant of the devil, the spirit of the devil enters him and takes possession of him: "And you hath he quickened, who were dead in trespasses and sins; wherein in time past ye walked according to the course of this world, according to the prince of the power of the air, the spirit that now worketh in the children of disobedience" (Eph. 2:1-2).

If the spirit of Satan enters a person, that spirit captures his mind and body so that he makes that person disobey God. Thus the person is made to turn his back on God and revolt against Him. And through the disobedience and confusion of the victim's mind, he comes to refuse the way of truth but chooses the broad way which leads to destruction.

We find it hard to convert an unbeliever and lead him or her to Jesus because an evil spirit in the mind and soul deceives that person. If we want to convert that one, we must first bind the indwelling evil spirit by our prayers. The Bible reads, "When a strong man armed keepeth his palace, his goods are in peace: but when a stronger than he shall come upon him, and overcome him, he taketh from him all his armour wherein he trusted, and divideth his spoils" (Luke 11:21-22).

"And the devil, taking him up into a high mountain, showed unto him all the kingdoms of the world in a moment of time. And the devil said unto him, All this power will I give thee, and the glory of them: for that is delivered unto me; and to whomsoever I will, I give it" (Luke 4:5-6).

Since all men who are dominated by original sin have become the servants of the devil and death, all of them are actually living under the unceasing control of the devil, even though they may prefer to be free of sin. The devil approaches us with the lust of the flesh, the lust of the eyes and the pride of life. Those who have become the servants of the devil struggle against the power of lust and live in fear and dread. Hebrews 2:14-15 reads, "That through death he might destroy him that had the power of death, that is, the devil; and deliver them, who through fear of death were all their lifetime subject to bondage." This passage shows us that Jesus came to loose those who were in bondage to the devil.

Judgment and the wrath of God are the final outcome for those who have become servants of the devil. With the death of man's spirit and the cessation of dialogue with God, man lost the fundamental knowledge which can discern the purpose and direction of his life. Since such a man depends solely on his human knowledge and experience, and is swayed by feelings and emotions, he decides to carry out everything from a selfish point of view. Since the soul of man always wants its way, man has become a thorough egotist. An example is Cain, who killed his brother, Abel. In the Bible we read, "For we wrestle not against flesh and blood, but against principalities, against powers, against the rulers of the darkness of this world, against spiritual wickedness in high places" (Eph. 6:12). Therefore, preaching is a spiritual struggle. The fact that we believe in Jesus is the proof that we have won in that spiritual battle.

One day a woman came to me for counsel about a problem with her child. In tears she told me: "Pastor, I have done my best for my son, and I do not think that I lack anything in my efforts to be a good mother. I give him an allowance which should be sufficient for his needs, but he leaves home often and takes some of our household goods to sell, saying that his allowance is not enough. Sometimes he does not come home for several days. He misses more school than he attends. I have rebuked him, but he is becoming violent, and all my efforts have been in vain. How can I solve this problem?''

"This problem has not come to you because your son is totally bad,''
I answered. "There is an evil spirit which has taken control of his soul
and is making him behave in this way. Since evil spirits do not go out
except by prayer and fasting, you must fast and pray to loose your son
from the bondage of the evil spirit. Then he will change.''

The power which drives numerous people into the pit of despair is the
spirit of Satan. It is the power which steals and destroys. Satan boasts
that all members of mankind since the fall of Adam have become his
servants. Because of greed, disputes arose which resulted in the bloody
history of wars among the nations as well as fighting between individuals.
Passion took the lead in every field of major human activities. Even sins
of taking human life in a whim of passion were committed. In Genesis
4:23 we see this frightening situation: "Adah and Zillah, hear my voice;
ye wives of Lamech, hearken unto my speech: for I have slain a man
to my wounding, and a young man to my hurt.''

Those who do not have faith in God live in a dissolute manner, bound
by the lust of the flesh much the same as animals, and will not escape
the judgment and wrath of God. The Bible tells us that the end of people
who disobey God will be violent because the evil that controls them will
be violent: "He that believeth on the Son hath everlasting life: and he
that believeth not on the Son shall not see life; but the wrath of God abideth
on him" (John 3:36). "But the fearful, and unbelieving, and the abominable, and murderers, and whoremongers, and sorcerers, and idolaters,
and all liars, shall have their part in the lake which burneth with fire
and brimstone: which is the second death" (Rev. 21:8). "For the wages
of sin is death" (Rom. 6:23). "And so death passed upon all men, for
that all have sinned" (Rom. 5:12).

People who live in the soulish realm reveal how weak pride is. When
God looked upon man, living according to the desires of his flesh, God
regretted that He had made him: "My spirit shall not always strive with
man, for that he also is flesh" (Gen. 6:3).

At the time of the flood, God destroyed all flesh except Noah's family.
They were still dead in spirit, however, so his descendants kept living
their self-centered lives without God. When they multiplied and became
strong, they began to build the tower of Babel, a symbol of their egotism:
"Go to, let us build us a city, and a tower, whose top may reach unto
heaven; and let us make us a name, lest we be scattered abroad upon
the face of the whole earth" (Gen. 11:4).

God saw their pride and judged them by confusing their language. People in this day live in their self-centered way, too, led by the lust of the flesh, the lust of the eyes and the pride of this world. Egotism which knows no compromise, with endless pride, excessive greed and the crimes which go along with selfishness, draw the wrath of God with fiery judgment which is closer than some think.

Many people who live in the soulish realm are living in torment, already being punished in the world. Evil instead of good, death instead of life, sorrow instead of joy, pain instead of pleasure, cold loneliness instead of warm relationship describe the hell they are living in now.

First, our Lord desired that our soul should prosper because our spirit was dead and the dialogue of love with God was cut off. Second, we have been driven out of the garden of blessing. Third, God has left our hearts and the devil has come in and enslaved us. Fourth, men whose spirits are dead and who live only by their soulish natures are judged already in the present. In the future they will face final judgment and be cast into the lake of fire.

God looks at such miserable human beings and calls them "Beloved!" This is the same voice of love which has called to us since the creation of the world. Such a God desires that our souls may prosper once again. With so much love that He did not spare His only begotten Son, He desires that our souls may prosper, that the creative order may be restored, that He may come into the vessels of our humanity and dwell therein. Like the old times when God walked with Adam and had conversations with him, today God intends to come into our hearts, to walk and talk with us, and to change our lives so that we will prosper and be in good health, even as our soul prospers. Then we will have life and that more abundantly. Just now He is standing at our heart's door, knocking. Shall we open the door?

Life for Dead Spirits

God said this concerning man, "For I have created him for my glory" (Is. 43:7). Therefore the ultimate goal of human life is to show God's glory and to give glory to God. After Adam and Eve ate the fruit of the tree of knowledge, they lost both the glory of God and their goal in life. "For as by one man's disobedience many were made sinners, so by the obedience of one shall many be made righteous" (Rom. 5:19).

Man became so heavily depressed over becoming the servant of the devil, he could not be made whole again by his own power or works. Man could never return to his original state. Education and politics could never restore him either. Humanism certainly can never restore him. We are all the sons of Adam. We need a Savior—Jesus Christ.

Believe in Jesus Christ

The name "Jesus" means savior. "And she shall bring forth a son, and thou shalt call his name Jesus: for he shall save his people from their sins" (Matt. 1:21).

The name "Christ" means anointed one. Kings and priests were specially ordained by anointing their heads with oil. Therefore Jesus Christ is our Savior, who saves us and becomes our King and High Priest.

"For the Son of man is come to seek and to save that which was lost" (Luke 19:10). "Even as the Son of man came not to be ministered unto, but to minister, and to give his life a ransom for many" (Matt. 20:28). Jesus came to save us. What must we do to be saved? Just come to God by faith, depending upon the power of His blood, and ask Him to save us and come into our lives.

We cannot come to God without the merit of the shed blood of Jesus (Lev. 17:11). We cannot be saved by the teaching of religion nor can we be saved by Christianity. We can only be forgiven and saved by the precious blood of Jesus. This is very clear in the Bible: "But if we walk in the light, as he is in the light, we have fellowship one with another, and the blood of Jesus Christ his Son cleanseth us from all sin" (1 John 1:7). "Forasmuch as ye know that ye were not redeemed with corruptible things, as silver and gold, from your vain conversation received by tradition from your father; but with the precious blood of Christ, as of a lamb without blemish and without spot" (1 Pet. 1:18,19).

Today many churches do not preach the blood of Jesus. They talk much about the teachings and the life of Jesus, but they neither bear witness to the blood of Jesus nor praise it. Sinners can neither be led to forgiveness nor be led to salvation without the blood of Jesus. Without faith in the precious blood, the worship service and ceremonies and rituals are empty. "Without shedding of blood, there is no remission [of sins]" (Heb. 9:22). The blood of Jesus makes it possible for us to communicate with Him. Therefore we can sing: "What can wash away my sin? Nothing but the blood of Jesus." Putting our trust in this blood, we can come into the presence of God. Trusting in this blood, we can win over the attacks of Satan. Relying on this blood, we can do good. When we apply the blood of Jesus Christ to our lives in creative confession, just as the children of Israel in the Old Testament placed the blood of the Passover lamb on their doors, the devil flees, frightened out of his senses. By believing in the redeeming blood of Jesus Christ, we experience the miracle of being saved. "For God so loved the world, that he gave his only begotten Son, that whosoever believeth in him should not perish, but have everlasting life" (John 3:16). "But these are written, that ye might believe that Jesus is the Christ, the Son of God; and that believing ye might have life through his name" (John 20:31).

The original Greek word for the life which we receive through our faith in Jesus Christ is *zoe*. This is the life which comes from God. By obtaining this faith our spirits can be renewed. In other words, the Greek word for the ordinary life in which the spirit is dead is *psuche*. This simply means our physical life. The new life, which we obtain by our confidence and trust in the blood of Jesus, is the life from God. When we have this life, our dead spirits become alive again.

Can all men be saved because Jesus died for us? Never. It is not so. As we have stated previously, we are saved by faith. Because Jesus died on the cross and rose again, breaking the power of Satan, we are judged when we do not believe the facts: "He that believeth on Him is not condemned: but he that believeth not is condemned already, because he hath not believed in the name of the only begotten Son of God" (John 3:18).

The Holy Spirit comes to the world and reproves the world of sin, and of righteousness, and of judgment, for mankind has not reached righteousness without believing in the redemption of Jesus Christ. The Bible shows that salvation is provided freely for everyone without discrimination. "And he said unto them, Go ye into all the world, and preach the gospel to every creature. He that believeth and is baptized shall be saved; but he that believeth not shall be damned" (Mark 16:15-16). "For God sent not his Son into the world to condemn the world; but that the world through him might be saved. He that believeth on Him is not redeemed: but he that believeth not is condemned already, because he hath not believed in the name of the only begotten Son of God" (John 3:17-18). "He that believeth on the Son hath everlasting life: and he that believeth not the Son shall not see life; but the wrath of God abideth on him" (John 3:36).

These scriptures show clearly that although Jesus was crucified and shed His blood for all, salvation can take effect only for the one who voluntarily accepts Jesus Christ as Savior. Those who do not accept Jesus have no hope. Therefore, in order to have salvation, eternal life and spirits that are made alive, first we must go through the totally personal process of receiving Jesus Christ as our personal Savior.

What will happen at the moment we believe in Jesus Christ and receive Him into our lives? What will the Holy Spirit do?

Be Born Again by the Holy Spirit

When we receive Jesus into our lives as our Savior and make Him the Lord of our lives, if we think we have done it "all by ourselves," we are missing the mark. It is written, "No man can say that Jesus is Lord but by the Holy Ghost" (1 Cor. 12:3). Therefore, in order that we may be saved and our spirits revived, the Holy Spirit must come to us and inspire and touch our hearts that they may be regenerated.

One evening Nicodemus, a ruler of the Jews, came to Jesus and asked Him how he could receive eternal life. Jesus answered and said to him that except a man be born again, he cannot see the kingdom of God. Nicodemus' thoughts were all focused on the words "born again," for Nicodemus had desired the kingdom of God all his life. Nicodemus, who knew he couldn't enter the second time into his mother's womb and be born all over again, could not understand what Jesus said. But Jesus replied to him, "Except a man be born of water and of the Spirit, he cannot enter into the kingdom of God. That which is born of the flesh is flesh; and that which is born of the Spirit is spirit. Marvel not that I said unto thee, Ye must be born again" (John 3:5-7).

By coming first to give us salvation and convict us of our sins, the Holy Spirit makes us recognize our situation and repent of our sins. He makes us realize that we are made righteous, not by our own deeds, but by the blood of Jesus Christ. By convicting us of judgment He makes us understand that the prince of this world, Satan, is already judged through the cross of Christ—and this helps us confess our sins and believe in Jesus Christ. Without the work of the Holy Spirit, we can neither receive salvation nor understand it.

All people are born of human parents and are therefore flesh. If we practice a religion, it must necessarily be a religious flesh. If we follow ethics and morality, we become moral and ethical flesh. If we receive a lot of education, we become educated flesh. Flesh is always flesh and cannot be changed into the spirit, so we cannot become the spiritual man until we are born again by the Holy Spirit and receive spiritual life.

To be born of the Holy Spirit means that the Holy Spirit comes in, dwells within us and becomes our master. Being freed from the bondage of Satan by believing in the death and resurrection of Jesus Christ is referred to as being "born again." We are thus changed from being slaves of the devil to being children of God. Because the Holy Spirit causes us to become children of God, we can call God our Father, and our spirits are revived by the Holy Spirit: "God hath sent forth the Spirit of his Son into your hearts, crying, Abba, Father" (Gal. 4:6). "For ye have not received the spirit of bondage again to fear; but ye have received the Spirit of adoption, whereby we cry, Abba, Father. The Spirit itself beareth witness with our spirit, that we are the children of God" (Rom. 8:15,16). "Now if any man have not the Spirit of Christ, he is none of his" (Rom. 8:9).

At the moment when the Holy Spirit comes to us and makes us admit that Jesus is our Lord, our dead spirits are revived from the sleep of death and born again. Then we cannot help being moved to tears of gratitude for the joy we receive at our rebirth. That we call God "Father" is not an ordinary experience. Only the person who has the indwelling Holy Spirit can call God "Father" with a deep, genuine feeling that He is truly Father. Only because the Holy Spirit has come into us, giving us the spirit of adoption and making us sons of God, are we able to call God our Father.

The Holy Spirit, who is the Spirit of Christ, presently continues the work of Jesus Christ in our lives. Through the Holy Spirit we can experience even now the presence and work of Christ.

Before ascending into heaven, Jesus gave us this wonderful promise: "Go ye therefore, and teach all nations, baptizing them in the name of the Father, and of the Son, and of the Holy Ghost: teaching them to observe all things whatsoever I have commanded you: and, lo, I am with you alway, even unto the end of the world" (Matt. 28:19-20). Jesus said also, "For where two or three are gathered together in my name, there am I in the midst of them" (Matt. 18:20).

Since Jesus ascended into heaven before the eyes of His disciples after He was crucified, dead and resurrected, He is no more present in this world in the bodily sense. In spite of that, our Lord promised that He would be with us. What does that mean? Through other sayings of Jesus we know that this promise is sincere.

"And I will pray the Father, and he shall give you another Comforter, that he may abide with you forever; even the Spirit of truth; whom the world cannot receive, because it seeth him not, neither knoweth him: but ye know him; for he dwelleth with you, and shall be in you." I will not leave you comfortless: I will come to you" (John 14:16-18).

What a wonderful scripture! This promises us that though Jesus would leave this world, He would send another Comforter to us, to stay with us. Here the ''Comforter'' is someone who is called to be always beside a person to help him. Yet Jesus called him ''another Comforter.'' The Greek word for ''other'' is *allos*, and this is the word used to signify another of the same thing. Thus the Holy Spirit is another Comforter which is like the first one. And Jesus said also: ''Howbeit when he, the Spirit of truth, is come, he will guide you into all truth: for he shall not speak of himself; but whatsoever he shall hear, that shall he speak: for he will show you things to come. He shall glorify me: for he shall receive of mine, and shall show it unto you'' (John 16:13-14).

This means that another Comforter, the Holy Spirit, will continue the work which Jesus began. Jesus is resurrected and now sits at the right hand of God the Father. The Holy Spirit, who is our Comforter, now comes to us and continues the work done by Jesus in the same way. The coming of the Holy Spirit continued the ministry of Jesus. The fullness of the Holy Spirit is the fullness of Jesus and the presence of the Holy Spirit is the presence of Jesus. Therefore, the Holy Spirit quickens our dead spirits just as Jesus raised the son of a widow in Nain. The Holy Spirit revives our spiritual life as Jesus raised Lazarus, thereby making us children of God. By bringing down the wall between man and God, the Holy Spirit enables us to renew spiritual dialogue with God. Through this work of the Holy Spirit we have been set free from the bondage of the devil and have come to experience the mystery of living in close fellowship with Jesus. The Bible says this clearly: ''Even when we were dead in sins, [God] hath quickened us together with Christ...and hath raised us up together, and made us sit together in heavenly places in Christ Jesus'' (Eph. 2:5-6).

God paid for our sins and forgave them through the blood of Jesus. By the resurrection of Jesus, God quickened us who were dead in our sins. Jesus rose again, not alone, but with us. Not only did Jesus live 2,000 years ago in the land of Judea, He is alive with us now. Therefore, you are now by no means alone, for Jesus is in you and you are in Jesus. From now on we all dwell together in unity as brothers. Therefore we who have Jesus Christ and have been bought by His blood have become brethren and have eternal life. ''Behold, how good and how pleasant it is for brethren to dwell together in unity...for there the Lord commanded the blessing, even life forevermore'' (Ps. 133:1-3). Becoming one with Him and with other brethren results in God's blessing and prospering our spiritual life.

The New Order

When our spirits are born again by the blood of Jesus Christ and by the work of the Holy Spirit, a new order, which changes our lives completely, is established. The soul that lived in sin in the past, not knowing that God was grieved because the dialogue with Him was severed, turns now from the path of sin. Our souls leap and rejoice when we know God loves us; but if God is sad, our souls are oppressed and tormented also. When you and I pray earnestly, we can feel God's answer to our prayer through the peace and conviction which comes to our hearts. When we hear the Word of God the response of our hearts is a hearty "Amen!" This is our dialogue with God through our spirits, and by this dialogue we realize clearly that our spirits are revived.

We who were driven out of the presence of God because of sin are now received into the presence of God. We were strangers and pilgrims like other people while we lived for this world. They are still strangers who do not know Jesus and wander aimlessly, but we have a clear goal because we are being led by the Holy Spirit.

Since our spirits have been made alive by the Holy Spirit, we now understand the Word when we hear a sermon or read the Scriptures. We can sing hymns, pray and communicate with God. The most important thing for us is that our spirits should be made alive. Mere religion will not do it. The celebration of rituals cannot do it. For our spirits to be made alive, we must meet Jesus Christ and accept Him as our Savior. Then the Holy Spirit, the Spirit of Christ, will breathe into our spirits and quicken them.

The fact that our spirits are now alive is proof that the Holy Spirit dwells within us. In the new order which is now in effect, since the Spirit of God is now within us, the bondage to Satan and his oppression has been broken and removed. Now our spirits are alive and begin to prosper. But we must go through the upheaval which was caused by the collapse of the old order. Our souls resist the change and there is pain. However, there is no reason to worry, because no matter how violently our souls may resist they are destined to obey our renewed spirits. If you are reading this book and have the conviction that the Holy Spirit dwells within, then He has become the Master of your life and the victory is yours!

The Resistance of the Soul

When Jesus broke the bondage of sin, a conflict began between the spirit and the soul. The flesh shouts, "You may as well go ahead and satisfy the carnal desires, because they must be satisfied anyway!" The spirit says, "No, we will live according to the Word of God." Then the battle is on! The soul cannot tolerate control by the spirit, because in the past the soul has always been the controlling force. Consequently, there is sharp competition and struggle for mastery between the soul and the spirit. We cannot see this struggle from the viewpoint of a bystander, but it is a very real struggle and it is going on in our hearts at this very moment. But now the sweet, fresh breath of the Holy Spirit is free to blow His breath of life into our spirits and we are enabled to live according to God's will. Our spirits now try to live according to the Word of God, worthy of the name "children of God." Even though we may suffer pain or misunderstanding, our spirits will still try to discern the will of God. The soul resists, saying, "Do you think you are the only conscientious person in the whole world? God will overlook your wrongdoing. This is your chance. Why not make the best of this opportunity?"

The soul tries to regain control in every way possible at every turn in the road, and the soul always wants to be in control from the standpoint of fleshly desires, not according to God's Word.

After our spirits are made alive, God will not wink at the arrogance of the soul. Though Jesus Christ may not concern Himself in the matters of those who live in the soulish realm, who serve Satan and seek carnal pleasures, He will never give up His children. He has purchased us with His blood! He will keep us! This is the love of God. If we give in to our souls' pleading and return to the direction our soulish nature would go in, we will have a rough time, for the Holy Spirit will follow wherever we go, pleading gently but firmly with us to return. Eventually we will have to go through the bitter experience of being broken, and that is painful.

God Breaks Our Soulish Natures

Among believers there are still many who have never been broken. Though they know clearly that if they live according to their spirit they can have life, peace and victory, their lack of faith in God often causes them to resort to the soulish way of life to which they have been accustomed for so long. These people cannot expect to experience a life of power and miracles. Their prayers will not be answered because the soul by no means can understand the work of God in the realm of the spirit.

Therefore God must break our soulish natures, so that He may prepare us for the miraculous life. We find that all the great servants of God in the Bible went through experiences of being broken. Let's take a look at several Bible examples of men who experienced brokenness before God.

Abraham is the father of the faith, as we all know. In spite of that, he had to live through the pain of being broken, an experience which cost him twenty-five years of life. God had commanded Abraham when he was seventy-five years old to get out of his country, away from his family and his father's house, and go to a land that God would show him (Gen. 12:1). But Abraham, full of human excuses, took along with him all his possessions and his nephew Lot.

A casual observer may think that Abraham obeyed the voice of God, but a close look at Scripture shows us that he disobeyed. God judged Abraham for his disobedience, his carnal desires. This disobedience brought about the famine which came to the land of Canaan at that time. Abraham was not aware that the famine had been caused by his disobedience, so he went down to Egypt to avoid it. In Egypt he went on his merry way, living to satisfy his soulish nature. When he entered the land, he lied about his relationship with his wife, saying she was his sister. He said he needed to lie to preserve his life. He was obeying the whispering of his soul. He knew in his spirit that not only his life but also blessing and cursing were in the hands of God. Yet, when he faced a crisis, he followed his soulish way because he had more experience in going his own way.

And that wasn't all. Abraham went on from bad to worse, experiencing shame and disgrace. He lied to Abimelech, the king of Gerar, and for the second time he said that his wife was his sister. This lie almost cost the king's life.

Even after all this, Abraham still did not separate himself from Lot. Wherever they went, there was quarrelling between his herdsmen and Lot's. For Abraham there was not one day without problems. This is typical of the person who follows the desires of the flesh. He lives a life full of anxiety without rest.

In the end, after much suffering, Abraham was broken. Only then did he separate himself from Lot. Falling down before God in repentance, he determined that from then on he would obey God and follow His leading. Then God gave them a son, Isaac, according to His earlier promise to Abraham.

Now let's take a look at Isaac. On the whole Isaac lived a very quiet life without many ups and downs. Yet God had to break him, too. When he was a youth he came very close to tasting death when his father took him up to Mount Moriah to offer a burnt offering to God. They prepared wood, but there was no lamb for the burnt offering. When Isaac asked

Abraham where the lamb was, Abraham answered, "God will provide himself a lamb for a burnt offering" (Gen. 22:8).

Since Isaac was a spiritual young man, he believed Abraham. He obeyed even to the last moment when his father bound him and lifted the hand which held the knife poised to kill him. Seeing such faith and obedience, God sent His angel and stopped Abraham, telling him to offer a ram which was caught in a thicket nearby. God rewarded Isaac's faith because he lived according to his spirit.

We can also look at Jacob, the son of Isaac. The name "Jacob" means a swindler or a crafty person. As he grew older he was vexed and tormented because he was not entitled to the birthright of the firstborn son. When his brother was faint with hunger, Jacob took advantage of him by exchanging food for his birthright. Then, because Isaac was old and blind and easily misled, Jacob successfully deceived his father, Isaac, and received the blessing which had been intended for Esau, his brother. Jacob followed the directions of his soulish nature from beginning to end. To avoid his brother's anger, Jacob ran away to the home of his uncle Laban. During the 20 years he lived with Laban he was deceived many times. He was reaping what he had sown. One night, without telling his uncle that he was leaving, he left with all his possessions.

When Jacob made up his mind to return home, he found that the journey was a difficult one. He learned that his estranged brother was coming to meet him with 400 men. But cunning Jacob took care of that matter by sending a handsome gift to Esau and then sat down on the bank of a brook.

We can imagine what must have been going through his mind. He realized the day of reckoning was near. Crafty Jacob sent the gifts to Esau. Then he sent all his animals and herds, wives and children and servants, hoping that his brother's anger would cool down. By the time they met he would have a better chance to save his own skin. Jacob was a man who lived by the dictates of his soulish nature.

At midnight, all alone on the bank of the brook with the uncomfortable memory of his deception, something happened. Suddenly a man appeared who wrestled with Jacob until daybreak. At first Jacob might have thought the man was an assassin sent by his brother Esau, but he soon realized that the man was an angel sent by God. When the angel saw that Jacob was determined to prevail, he struck the sinew of the hollow of Jacob's thigh, putting it out of joint and making it impossible for Jacob to run. He had to stay and face Esau. When Jacob saw that he had lost the wrestling match, he clung to the angel in desperation, saying, "I will not let thee go, except thou bless me" (Gen. 32:26). In this struggle, Jacob's soulish nature was completely broken.

Jacob represents the soul, and the angel of God represents the spirit. When the soul surrendered to the spirit, the soul then had to submit to the spirit. Jacob was a crafty swindler who had lived a life directed by his soul, but now Scripture tells us that Jacob was broken so that God could use him. Indeed Isaiah says that when Jacob became thus broken, God used him to bring a great nation into being—Israel!

The Bible's description is apt: "Fear not, thou worm Jacob, and ye men of Israel; I will help thee, saith the Lord, and thy Redeemer, the Holy One of Israel. Behold, I will make thee a new sharp threshing instrument having teeth: thou shalt thresh the mountains, and beat them small, and shalt make the hills as chaff" (Is. 41:14-15).

What is there about a worm that could resemble Jacob's life? A worm is helpless. It cannot see or hear, and it is at the mercy of anyone passing by. In Jacob's desperate hour of fighting for survival for his family and himself, when he did not know whether Esau would kill him or not, Jacob threw himself at the mercy of the angel and allowed himself to be broken and subdued. When he was broken, God turned the situation around for him and restored him to his brother.

Jacob's son, Joseph, was also a man who went through the process of being completely broken. In the Bible, Joseph was the most innocent man with the least amount of human sinfulness. Yet Joseph had a strong soul, for though his life was praiseworthy, and he had a dream in his heart, the boasting of his dream to his parents and his brothers was the behavior of a self-centered person.

Before God made Joseph's dream come true, he also had to go through some astonishing hardships which kept getting worse. His brothers came very close to killing him, but they decided instead to sell him to some Midianite merchants as a slave. In Egypt Joseph was purchased by Potiphar and became the overseer over Potiphar's house and business, because he worked faithfully and diligently.

But then Joseph ran into problems with his master's wife and landed in the king's prison, a place which had the reputation of being such a horrible place of punishment that it was the last place one could expect to come out alive. In the royal prison Joseph's soul was completely broken. At last he became a spiritual man. Though he still kept his dream, he did not boast about it.

Then Joseph was suddenly and dramatically promoted to ruler over all the people in Egypt. Just as had been foretold in his dreams, his eleven brothers came and prostrated themselves before him. When his elder brothers trembled in fear and begged him to forgive them, he comforted them saying: "Fear not: for am I in the place of God? But as for you, ye thought evil against me; but God meant it unto good, to bring to pass, as it is this day, to save much people alive. Now therefore fear ye not: I will nourish you, and your little ones" (Gen. 50:19-21).

Another man whose soul was broken, for God to use him greatly, was Moses. Adopted by the daughter of Pharaoh, who dominated the world of that day, and brought up in the luxurious style of the palace, Moses received the excellent education of a prince. He was tutored in literary and military arts. He was well versed in every area of learning. Nevertheless, deep in his heart he knew that he was an Israelite, belonging to the people of God, and that he must in some way see his people delivered from their slavery.

When Moses reached 40 years of age, he thought the time had come to lead his people to deliverance. One day he went to the area where his brethren worked. Seeing a terrible situation there, he killed an Egyptian taskmaster and buried him in the sand. Because of this he was forced to escape to the desert because Pharaoh now sought his life.

In the land of Midian he married Zipporah and reared a family, living an ordinary life of a shepherd for 40 years. Just as Jacob was so broken that he was described as an earthworm, so Moses was broken in the desert of Midian to become the servant which God could use mightily. His spirit was so broken that he almost died. His soulish nature, including his temper and the humanistic learning gained in his Egyptian upbringing, were gradually disappearing.

After a long period of suffering, one day Moses heard the voice of God as he watched a bush burning on Mount Horeb. God spoke from the bush: "I will send thee unto Pharaoh, that thou mayest bring forth my people the children of Israel out of Egypt" (Ex. 3:10).

Moses fell on his face and said, "Who am I, that I should go unto Pharaoh, and that I should bring forth the children of Israel out of Egypt?" (Ex. 3:11).

In the past, Moses had been forward in settling things for himself, but during the 40 years of living in the desert, his soul was so broken that he became a humble man. God could not use him until this had come about.

Not only in the Old Testament, but also in the New Testament, God first allowed His prospective servants to experience brokenness.

One day Jesus took His disciples to the Sea of Galilee. The weather was fine and the lake was calm. Jesus told His disciples to go to the other side of the lake. This word of Jesus was the Word of God, the creator, God who made the heavens and the earth and everything in them. If Jesus said it, it would happen, and nothing in all of nature could stop the process. But the disciples were people who depended on their feelings for direction. They were people who put their trust in what they could see, rather than putting their trust in what Jesus told them.

When their little ship came to the middle of the lake, there suddenly arose a storm. On the Sea of Galilee, a temporary vacuum can form on the water by the wind blowing from Mount Hermon, because the lake is 600 feet below sea level. When a storm broke suddenly on that body of water, great waves arose that were impossible for a small boat to escape unless it did so within half an hour. When the disciples' boat came to the midst of the lake, the wind began to blow from Mount Hermon and waves arose on the lake.

The disciples fought hard to make the best of their knowledge and experience, but before long they became tired and water began to fill the boat in spite of their desperate efforts to bail it out. The boat, and even the oars with which they were rowing, were broken. Now they were helpless, and shipwreck seemed only a step away. The disciples were so frightened that they did not know what to do next. It was then that they turned to Jesus, who was sleeping, and cried, "Lord, save us: we perish." Then Jesus commanded the waves, saying, "Peace, be still" (Matt. 8:25; Mark 4:39).

The sea suddenly became calm at the command of Jesus. If the disciples had awakened Jesus a little earlier, their trouble could have ended earlier, but since they decided to use their own human ability, they had a difficult time until they reached the end of their human resources. Since Jesus had told the disciples, "Let us [plural] go over to the other side," they should have gone in dependence on His Word, regardless of the change of circumstances. As we realize that Jesus was Master of the winds and the waves, we know that He would not have sunk with the ship. Neither would He have allowed the disciples to go down. What a beautiful truth! When Jesus is in us, we can truly know that we will not go down in the storms of life, because He is at the helm and is still the Master of every situation if we trust Him completely.

At another time Jesus startled His disciples when He allowed them to experience panic in a situation with a man who had an unclean spirit, and again when He ordered them to feed more than 5,000 people. From the death of Jesus until His resurrection, the souls of the disciples were so thoroughly broken that they fell into despair. Through these experiences Jesus was training His disciples to lean on Him, casting aside all human reasoning in order to become spiritual disciples. Jesus trained Paul by this method, as He has trained all those who have gone before us throughout 2,000 years of Christian history. All these men of faith were used by God only after they had experienced brokenness.

Although God answers our prayer, blessing and prospering us after we are born again, He also does a work of breaking us so that we may have even greater blessing. The deeper our faith becomes, the more we have experiences that challenge us to allow God to break us, but the more we experience brokenness, the deeper our faith becomes. We should never think that we have been totally broken and that we will never go through a breaking period again. No, we can never say we have "arrived." God breaks our soulish natures endlessly because He wants to bestow endless blessings on us. God will cause us, being broken, to stop acting like the masters of our lives but He will bring us to a place of living in the Spirit in humble obedience to Him.

From One Vessel to Another Vessel

Through the process of making wine, we find an example of how God works to break our self-centeredness in the realm of the soul. When wine is made, the grapes are mashed and the juice of the grapes is all mixed up with the dregs. After placing the juice in a big vessel, it is poured several times from one vessel to another. All the dregs eventually settle during this process. The fragrant, delicious juice which is pure and transparent becomes separated from the dregs.

God prepares us to bring glory to His name through the vessels of tribulation and hardship, by the process of pouring us from one vessel to another. He removes all the "dregs" in our character and in our faith through this method. These vessels signify various hardships that we encounter on our path of life. Let us look at the vessels which God prepares for us.

First, there is the vessel of misunderstanding. We may be born again and believing in Jesus and even having joy in our hearts, but many dregs may still remain in our character. We will then become egocentric, easily irritated, worldly, and fall into lustfulness and debauchery. But when we come to God with the attitude, "Father, I stretch out my hands to Thee, no other help I know," then God pours us from our present vessel into the vessel of misunderstanding in order to remove these dregs.

This vessel of being misunderstood has a hue. People, who so often judge things by the outward color rather than the contents, frequently misunderstand us. We lament or complain, but we must bear all these things obediently, for God has poured us into this vessel of misunderstanding to get rid of the dregs in our life. The more we struggle, the more the dregs will stir and come to the surface, only to make our stay in the vessel of misunderstanding longer. Therefore, when we undergo hardship by being misunderstood, we should not struggle to get out of it. We should bear and endure it obediently until we let the dregs settle. When we pray and wait without complaining, all the misunderstanding will clear up. Thus in this vessel of misunderstanding we can allow the drops of self-centeredness, hatred, doubt, impatience, anxiety and stubbornness settle.

When we reach this stage, misunderstandings by others are cleared up in no time and we feel free as a bird in the sky. However, this only continues for a short period and then our Lord pours us into another vessel.

The second vessel is the vessel of trial. The first vessel had a transparent hue, but this one is a brownish-black glazed pottery vessel with a narrow neck and a round, wide bottom. All is pitch-dark inside. We feel choked because we see no light. Maybe the family is on the verge of divorce, or the business is shaken from its foundation and no plans work smoothly. We can only see darkness ahead of us and we are in the depths of despair. We can do nothing but sigh because everything is dark.

In the darkness of our situation we go to the church and hear the sermon of the pastor: "Stand on the word of promise which shall in no wise pass away, not one jot or tittle until heaven and earth pass away. We must live according to God's Word, even though we may see nothing and hear nothing and touch nothing, while in front of us there is only pitch-darkness. God's Word works miracles every day."

When we hear these words, we are comforted and we can endure and wait in the dark vessel of trial. Our faith grows little by little while we grab hard at the words of promise in the Bible from Genesis to Revelation, regardless of our physical environment and surroundings. We have the attitude of mind that "man shall not live by bread alone, but by every word that proceedeth out of the mouth of God" (Matt. 4:4). Here the dregs of unbelief and impatience settle.

Passing through the second vessel, the wine has become much purer. Now we can see our image reflected clearly in the wine as in a mirror. We give out the fragrance of the Lord in our character. People say about us, "That person's life, speech and behavior have changed." Then our Lord pours us from the pottery vessel into another vessel.

The third vessel is the vessel of devotion or "ministering unto the Lord." The vessel of devotion is shallow and wide like the lid of a crock. In this vessel we can see what our devotion or our "ministering unto the Lord" looks like in His eyes and in the eyes of others who observe our everyday living in the light of what we profess. We are able to see how much or little we give ourselves to prayer to become like Him. The comments of others evoke humility or pride. Then we see just how pure or impure our worship really is. After a time we can bear no more, and we stretch out our hands to the Lord and cry, "Lord, I cannot live a good, righteous life by myself. Hold me with the strength and power of the Holy Spirit."

We realize that we cannot make our devotional life successful without the help of Jesus. Though we are sinful and vile enough to deserve hell, by the precious blood of Jesus we are forgiven all transgressions. We must get rid of the avarice and idolatry that lingers in our hearts by the purifying fire of the Holy Spirit. Finally, we reach the conclusion that the only power that can enable us to stand as people of God and before a lost and dying world is the power of the Holy Spirit.

In this world there is no one who can make his devotional life successful solely by his own will, discipline and moral ability. Today we deacons, elders and even pastors seem to be well behaved and respectable, but in ways unseen to the church we commit all kinds of secret sins and allow corrupt thinking in our minds. Our transgressions have been forgiven, but we cannot control our sinful lusts because we don't exercise the power which the Holy Spirit gives every believer. In order to lead a consistent devotional life, whether anyone is observing it or not, it is necessary to have the fullness of the Holy Spirit. Then boastfulness and our own will settles in this vessel of devotion. The Holy Spirit then monitors our behavior and leads us into a deeper experience with Christ through the fullness of the Spirit.

The fourth vessel which we are poured into by divine providence is the vessel of guidance. This vessel is shaped like a trumpet, so it has a winding configuration. Once we are poured into this vessel, we begin to feel that we can't see the direction of our lives because of the winding way in which we are led. Through our stay in this vessel we will be taught about the providence of the Holy Spirit, our guide.

In the past we lived by human ways and means, with our soulish desires as the center of our existence, following the direction of human wisdom and reason. But since we now have devoted ourselves to God and have been filled with the Holy Spirit, we find ourselves winding in and out of new experiences to find the will of the Lord. Sometimes we grope for our way as blind men touch an elephant, because we are not quite sure of the will of God. In the morning, we seem to know His will, at lunch time it seems that we don't, and in the evening the will of the Lord seems unclear again. The uncertainty of knowing which decision to make or what to do makes it appear that our confidence is wavering, because everything seems unfamiliar and new. And to make things worse, other Christians will make "helpful comments" such as "It seems to be that you are on the wrong track" or "Maybe something went wrong and you just failed to find God's will in this situation."

So we fall on our knees and pray, "Lord, I can't find my way. I commit my life, my heart, my body and my living to you. Please help me. You take the responsibility and take care of me."

When we pray like this, the earnestness of our prayer makes pride and greed seem unimportant. Then all the dregs of human pride, greed, anxiety and fear settle in the vessel of providence. Then the Holy Spirit comes to reveal His path and lead us to *His* will, not ours. At this point wonderful miracles happen, surpassing our human imagination!

In order to make good wine out of us, God prepares various vessels for us to pass through so that the dregs of our souls settle to the bottom of those vessels, thus bringing forth His best in us. Sometimes a husband becomes a vessel and sometimes a wife becomes one. Sometimes our in-laws, our neighbors and our relatives even play that role; at other times an illness or our business becomes a vessel.

When God pours us from vessel to vessel, He is breaking us and cleansing us more and more. He has His plan for us in mind. We must not look upon the problems we face but we must keep our eyes on God, the One who is working in our lives and who allowed us to be in this vessel. When we run into trials, misfortune, hardships and difficulties, we must remember that these are things which God allowed for expanding our spiritual growth. When trials, distress, pain and tribulation come, just pray calmly, bear the trials and persevere. Let us remember that we gave God permission to do whatever is necessary to make us fit for His glory and power, and He is doing just that. "And we know that all things work together for good to them that love God, to them who are called according to his purpose" (Rom. 8:28).

After we have been poured from one vessel to another we become sensitively enabled to discipline our inner man so that God can use us.

Discipline Your Soul

When we have experienced the breaking of our soulish nature, we must not be satisfied with that experience but allow the Holy Spirit to continue to teach us. The soul must be *disciplined* and trained to follow the leading of the Lord day by day. The Bible outlines for us what we must do after our breaking period: "And be not conformed to this world: but be ye transformed by the renewing of your mind, that ye may prove what is that good, and acceptable, and perfect will of God" (Rom. 12:2). In this scripture God requires that we must please Him and not follow the tendency of pleasing ourselves. We must obey the orders God gives us by His Spirit.

What is the best book which can train our souls? It is the Bible, for the Bible was not written "by the will of man: but holy men of God spake as they were moved by the Holy Ghost" (2 Pet. 1:21). "The word of God is quick, and powerful, and sharper than any two-edged sword, piercing even to the dividing asunder of soul and spirit, and of the joints and marrow, and is a discerner of the thoughts and intents of the heart" (Heb. 4:12).

God's Word is the spiritual food that we must eat in order to be able to discipline our souls. We are newborn babies whose spirits have been born again by the blood of Jesus Christ and the changing power of the Holy Spirit. "But as many as received him, to them gave he power to become the sons of God, even to them that believe on his name: which were born, not of blood, nor of the will of the flesh, nor of the will of man, but of God" (John 1:12-13).

Newborn babies become weakened or die unless they are fed with milk. Spiritual milk, which we spiritual babies should drink, is the Word of God. The apostle Peter exhorts us that we should lay aside all the habits of our carnal minds (souls) and eat the word so that our faith may grow to full measure. "Wherefore laying aside all malice, and all guile, and hypocrisies, and envies, and all evil speakings, as newborn babes, desire the sincere milk of the word, that ye may grow thereby" (1 Pet. 2:1-2).

We should by all means read the Bible, the Word of God, and live in obedience to it that we may grow as the children of God.

Jesus is the incarnate Word: "In the beginning was the Word, and the Word was with God, and the Word was God" (John 1:1). "And the Word was made flesh, and dwelt among us, (and we beheld his glory, the glory as of the only begotten of the Father), full of grace and truth" (John 1:14).

All of the recorded Word in the Bible from Genesis to Revelation is in some way the body of Jesus Christ. When the Israelites ate the Passover lamb in Egypt, they ate all the parts of the lamb: head, legs, all of it. When we read and meditate upon the 66 books of the Bible regularly, it is the same as if we eat the flesh of Jesus Christ. Our Lord suffered the tearing of His flesh in shedding His blood for us. His blood redeemed us who had been the slaves of the devil. His flesh became the bread of life which made us whole. "I am that bread of life" (John 6:48). "I am the living bread which came down from heaven: if any man eat of this bread, he shall live forever: and the bread that I will give is my flesh, which I will give for the life of the world" (John 6:51).

As we read the Word of God and meditate upon it, we are being changed into a beautiful character little by little, and our souls are becoming whole. We receive new strength and life as we march on boldly until we reach heaven's gate.

The soul does not come under subjection easily, even though it has been broken several times. At every possible opportunity the soul tries to gain mastery over our lives again so that we will return to our secular-human selfish ways against the will of God. Time and time again the soul raises questions before God and tries to have its own way, giving priority to reason. When we read the Scriptures during this time, the light of salvation written in the Word keeps us from falling into sin. The Bible says it in this way: "Thy word have I hid in mine heart, that I might not sin against thee" (Ps. 119:11), and "Thy word is a lamp unto my feet, and a light unto my path" (Ps. 119:105). When we read the Bible daily and live according to the Word, the Word becomes a lamp unto our path. It not only keeps us from failure, but it helps us to be victorious and defeat Satan who would try to devour us.

The Word of God is also like water. It cleanses us from all sin. Thus the Bible says, "That he might sanctify and cleanse it with the washing of water by the word" (Eph. 5:26). "Now are ye clean through the word which I have spoken unto you. Abide in me" (John 15:3-4).

When Jesus said to Nicodemus, "Except a man be born of water and of the Spirit, he cannot enter into the kingdom of God," this water referred to the Word of God. When we read the Scriptures, we realize that our hearts are full of unbelief and disobedience, but when we repent and are cleansed by the Word, we feel cleansed as if we had been washed by water. We are made clean in our hearts and lives because, through the Holy Spirit, the Lord is in us and we are in the Lord. The Bible says, "All scripture is given by inspiration of God, and is profitable for doctrine, for reproof, for correction, for instruction in righteousness" (2 Tim. 3:16).

After receiving this Word our souls do not resist, but they obey the Holy Spirit unconditionally. When such an order is established, the blessing of God comes to us.

So far we have learned the process or the way in which our soul can prosper. Our souls are broken only when they are put to the test so severely that they become totally lost as to what to do. Therefore, dearly beloved saints, don't be afraid when you encounter harsh difficulties. God is breaking your soul to make you live a spiritual life. He is pouring you from one vessel into another to remove the dregs and make more room for more blessing. Therefore, when you have a bitter experience, persevere and wait. The comfort of the Holy Spirit will come to you along with all other blessings.

The relationship between God and man is the relationship between the creator and things created. So it is like the relationship between the potter and the clay. While the potter has the power to make whatever he pleases, the clay must always submit and obey. The clay cannot argue with the potter. The relationship between God and man is the same. Man must absolutely obey the will of God and may not challenge it.

Man who lives by the direction of his carnal mind is characterized by sensualism, rationalization and egotism. He is a pleasure seeker and a slave to emptiness and death. Such a person laughs if he feels well, and is easily disappointed. When he has a little money to spare, he just spends it freely like water, but if his financial state turns a little, he complains.

The man whose soul has been broken, however, lives according to and depending upon the Word of God, and he centers his life in God. Though he meets with difficulty in everyday living, he stands on the Word of God. He may see no proof, hear no voice or touch anything with his hands, and in front of him there may be only pitch-black darkness. Yet he still walks boldly by faith with confidence. Moreover, he disciplines all his thinking and submits it to Christ.

When our spirits are quickened and we begin to pray, after our carnal mind has been broken, we become more like Jesus Christ. "Like a tree planted by the rivers of water," we will bring forth fruit in due season.

What is left of our soulish nature now? Once the soul is broken, we don't have to worry about our flesh. The flesh is now merely a paper tiger which has lost its ability to destroy us. We shall now see how to deal with the flesh.

Nailing the Flesh to the Cross

The body has its own consciousness of the world which it perceives through its senses. If it were not for the body, we could not perceive the world. Representing this bodily flesh is desire, and excessive desire turns into greed. Then sin enters with the devil. Lamenting such lust of the flesh, the apostle Paul cried, "O wretched man that I am! Who shall deliver me from the body of this death?" (Rom. 7:24).

If a man lives for lust, sin enters his heart and the devil follows it: "He that committeth sin is of the devil; for the devil sinneth from the beginning" (1 John 3:8).

Lust, sin and the devil are the trinity of evil. Where there is lust there is sin, and where there is sin there is the devil. As proof of this, death of the flesh follows. Our flesh can neither be broken nor trained like our souls, because it does not have comprehension. It acts on impulse. It can neither be persuaded nor corrected by discipline and training. If our sexual desire is aroused, we are likely to commit fornication. If the lust for drinking stirs within, we may abandon ourselves to drunkenness and dissipation. The flesh can ever be educated.

How then can the flesh be controlled? There is no way to control the flesh, except to nail it to the cross and destroy it. After realizing this fact the apostle Paul lamented, "O wretched man that I am" (Rom. 7:24), and confessed that he crucified himself daily. "I am crucified with Christ: nevertheless I live; yet not I, but Christ liveth in me: and the life which I now live in the flesh I live by the faith of the Son of God, who loved me, and gave himself for me" (Gal. 2:20). "I protest by your rejoicing which I have in Christ Jesus our Lord, I die daily" (1 Cor. 15:31).

The apostle Paul emphasizes in several scriptures that we should be nailed to the cross with Christ: "Knowing this, that our old man is crucified with him, that the body of sin might be destroyed, that henceforth we should not serve sin" (Rom. 6:6). "For if ye live after the flesh, ye shall die: but if ye through the Spirit do mortify the deeds of the body, ye shall live" (Rom. 8:13). "And they that are Christ's have crucified the flesh with the affections and lusts" (Gal. 5:24).

Thus the apostle Paul shows that the goal of the flesh is to honor Jesus: "But that with all boldness, as always, so now also Christ shall be magnified in my body, whether it be by life, or by death'' (Phil. 1:20).

Nowhere in the Bible can we find a passage admonishing us that our flesh should be trained and disciplined. We only find passages that teach us to nail our flesh to the cross! How can we nail the fleshly lusts and desires to the cross? There are three solutions in the Bible. The first solution is that we nail our flesh to the cross with Jesus Christ when we are baptized in water. The meaning of baptism is that our past self which lived a life of bondage unto death is nailed to the cross and we, as newborn creatures, live with Christ.

The Bible clearly shows us this fact: "Know ye not, that so many of us as were baptized into Jesus Christ were baptized into his death? Therefore we are buried with him by baptism into death: that like as Christ was raised up from the dead by the glory of the Father, even so we also should walk in newness of life'' (Rom. 6:3-4). "Buried with him in baptism, wherein also ye are risen with him through the faith of the operation of God, who hath raised him from the dead'' (Col. 2:12). So we see that through water baptism, we can nail our fleshly lusts and desires to the cross.

The second solution is to nail our flesh to the cross by receiving the baptism of the Holy Spirit. The Holy Spirit consumes all our lusts and sins, because the Holy Spirit is fire and baptizes with fire. Therefore, in order to destroy the sinful desires of the heart, we must be filled with the Holy Spirit.

The third solution is to extinguish our lusts and desires by fasting and prayer. Recently I received a letter from a young man which read as follows: "Pastor, I have been captured by the spirit of lewdness. I have spent all my earned money in a brothel, and my bondage also cost me much pain. In order to get delivered from this temptation and pain, I visited the church and the temple. I have done everything I could do by human means, but I only ended in despair. The spirit of lewdness drove me so hard it almost ruined me.

"Then recently someone persuaded me to come to the Yoido Full Gospel Church. So I came and listened to the sermon on fasting and prayer. When hearing the sermon that 'this kind goes not out but by fasting and prayer,' I fasted and prayed to break the spirit of lewdness and as soon as I did, the spirit went out. Now life is wonderful again. During this year, not one filthy thought has entered my mind, and I have not gone even once to a bawdy house. I have brought all my earnings home. I feel a great joy and freshness in my heart.''

People are still distressed today by lusts which drive them. Human lusts are like a thief who robs and intimidates, driving man to sinful places. These are the "bands of wickedness." Fasting and prayer are the only way to break these bands of wickedness and set man free from his oppressed condition. "Is not this the fast that I have chosen? To loose the bands of wickedness, to undo the heavy burdens, and to let the oppressed go free, and that ye break every yoke?" (Is. 58:6).

Where can we find a better weapon to mortify the flesh? The bands of wickedness, the heavy burden and the oppression—all these have their origin in fleshly lusts instigated by Satan.

To man, the most basic need is for food. Other desires can be ignored or postponed for a while, but in the case of hunger, it is impossible for him to put this off. There is an old Korean saying: "There is no one who can resist the temptation to break into another's house if he has been starving for three days."

When we abstain from eating food and pray, the power of Satan is utterly broken and our lusts fade away. Consequently, lay Christians as well as those who are specially called to the ministry should practice fasting often and thereby mortify fleshly lusts. Like the apostle Paul, they should die daily.

Some Christians say that they cannot afford the time needed to fast. In that case, they might avail themselves of the kind of fast that continues only during the daylight hours when the sun is in the sky. This fast is practiced in this way: It is kept during the three daytime meals—breakfast, lunch and supper—and is broken lightly with a light meal around ten o'clock at night. This is continued for three days—a fast of the three daytime meals and a light meal around ten o'clock at night. This type of fast has a great effect. People who work or businessmen who cannot afford to leave their businesses to visit a prayer mountain such as we have in Korea can fast this way.

During the daylight hours people are most easily swayed by the devil's temptations. By fasting during the daylight hours we can mortify the flesh. Yet we need to understand that there is no way to mortify the flesh once and for all. The apostle Paul said that he *died daily*. We must nail our fleshly lusts to the cross of Jesus Christ through fasting and prayer and rise again with Him to eternal life.

The Person Who Is Filled With the Holy Spirit

In this chapter we have seen how the person whose soul prospers looks at life. The fall of Adam brought death to man's spirit and his communion with God was severed. Man lived in sin, manipulated by the devil like a puppet. But by the merit of the precious blood of Jesus Christ, his sins were forgiven and his spirit was quickened by the Holy Spirit. The first grace we received when we entered the first room with the sign, "As Your Soul Prospers," was the grace of salvation.

After breaking our soulish nature, we learned to obey the direction and guidance of the Holy Spirit. The breaking period was painful and difficult, but through that painful process our faith grew and our understanding of the providence of God deepened. We learned that the secret of successfully nailing our flesh to the cross was found through fasting and prayer. By nailing ourselves daily to the cross we can learn the secret of full obedience to the leading of the Holy Spirit.

Day by day we realize that we have undergone a drastic change. We are totally different from the day when we accepted Jesus as our Savior. Now our speech, our acts and our whole being reveal the image of Jesus. We exude the fragrance of Jesus. People can tell we have been with Him. We speak and act like Him. Whereas we lived in the flesh before, gratifying our desires, we now live in the Spirit. Though we may see nothing and touch nothing in the spiritual realm, and though we possibly do not fully understand the way of the Holy Spirit, yet we go forward boldly with the faith that we are being led by Him.

We now lead a life with the Holy Spirit in control. And yet we can be controlled even more by the Holy Spirit. The *fullness* of the Holy Spirit means an overflowing experience resulting in two effects in our lives. The fullness of the Holy Spirit includes: 1) speaking in other tongues under the control of the Holy Spirit as a sign that we have received the fullness of the Holy Spirit; 2) an overflowing blessing which touches the lives of others as we live for Him. Speaking in other tongues, under the control of the Holy Spirit, does not necessarily mean that we are full of the Holy Spirit at all times.

When we receive the fullness of the Holy Spirit we share our overflowing experience with others throughout every day. In order to be *full* of the Holy Spirit we must be filled daily, and we can be. When the Holy Spirit grips our lives with His gentle but firm control, He also controls our tongues to speak in other languages which we never learned. At the same time our lives overflow with His blessing which we share with others everyday. When these two things occur, we can say we have the fullness of the Holy Spirit. When the Holy Spirit speaks through us in a language we never learned, He is glorifying Jesus through our lips, and the fruit of this wonderful experience is that we bless others with the blessing we receive. This is the new order. If that new order is established in our lives, nothing shall be impossible for us.

The threefold blessings which we are now learning about are primarily for our spiritual prosperity, in order that we should become good vessels to be used for a good purpose by a good God. This is the message of the full gospel and the first message of the threefold blessings of Christ.

A few years ago I was greatly impressed by the testimony of a cell-group leader in our church. This cell leader had a brother who had become a vegetable. He was alive but without the normal functions of recognizing, responding or caring, because of mental illness which claimed him more than ten years before. The condition of the patient was so acute that his family was forced to send him to a sanitorium. Then they forgot him.

Meanwhile, his sister accepted Jesus and received salvation and later became a deaconess. When she prayed, the Holy Spirit poured love into her heart with the conviction that her brother could be delivered from his mental disorder if he were taken from the sanitorium. She held a family meeting and proposed that her brother should be brought home. At first, the other family members were reluctant. They were worried that his illness would recur if he returned home.

But the deaconess believed God for a miracle. She prayed all night and waited for an answer from God. The answer came to her heart: "According to your faith be it unto you." Obeying the voice that was ringing in her heart, the deaconess brought her brother back home for the first time in ten years.

Then she invited our ministers to go to her home to pray for him. Miraculously, her brother was healed and restored completely just as if he had been awakened from a deep sleep. It was a phenomenon beyond human comprehension! Now the man attends our church regularly. He is very healthy and able and manages a farm!

How could such a thing happen? Those who live on an earthly level, in the flesh, can neither experience a miracle nor understand it. But a person whose spirit, soul and body have been recovered by the new order, whose spirit has been restored and who is full of the Holy Spirit can experience the world of miracles.

He whose soul prospers, reigns with Jesus Christ. While unbelievers serve the devil, Christians reign in new life. "Much more they which receive abundance of grace and of the gift of righteousness shall reign in life by one, Jesus Christ" (Rom. 5:17).

Now we are not afraid of death. While some people are afraid, believers consider it a joyful experience to think about going to be with Jesus, since heaven is their home and their hearts are already there.

Also, we are kings! Kings rule. As kings, we are given the power to rule and take dominion over our circumstances. We have been given authority over all power of the enemy. So we take our authority and drive out Satan in the powerful name of Jesus. We can now do mighty acts. So we take our authority and do them in the powerful name of Jesus: "And these signs shall follow them that believe; in my name shall they cast out devils" (Mark 16:17).

We are able to cast out devils. So we cast them out in the powerful name of Jesus, and they go—screaming! We have the power to resist the devil. So we resist him in the powerful name of Jesus: "Resist the devil, and he will flee from you" (James 4:7).

This is the Word of God to you and me! We are no longer ordinary people! We are citizens of heaven who possess eternal life and His power, which He shared with us. The devil will run at our command, and we shall bear in our lives the fruit of the Spirit: love, joy, peace, longsuffering, gentleness, goodness, faith, meekness and temperance.

If we are kings, shouldn't we have majesty, honor and material things befitting kings? This is our natural inheritance. It is a legacy which we can claim by showing the proper credentials. These are our treasures which we can claim as easily as we would draw money from a bank in which a generous amount of money had been deposited in our name with our account number on it. If one professes to be a king, but is impoverished and helplessly sick in bed, how can people believe he is a king?

3

That You May Prosper

herefore if any man be in Christ, he is a new creature: old things are passed away; behold, all things are become new" (2 Cor. 5:17). "Behold, I make all things new" (Rev. 21:5). "But ye are a chosen generation, a royal priesthood, a holy nation, a peculiar people" (1 Pet. 2:9).

God made us new in Christ and made us a royal priesthood. Consequently, if our spirits, souls and bodies prosper, it naturally follows that everything will go well. This is the order and the law of creation. Therefore it is not proper that a Christian should live a life which sees no success, unless God has a special purpose for withholding provision from him. God has chosen us as His royal priesthood so we will show forth the goodness and mercy of "him who hath called you out of darkness into his marvelous light" (1 Pet. 2:9). Why does God want others to look at us? It is to help others to come into the same blessings through the shed blood of Jesus. Therefore a Christian's life which is always full of failure is not a life which pleases God.

Korean churches take a vague attitude toward this teaching that a Christian should live a prosperous life. Some preachers do not speak out clearly on this point. Someone has said it is a Christian virtue to persevere in all things and endure when painful things come. The Korean Christian faith cannot shake off the impression that our religion emphasizes that we should grit our teeth and refrain from taking authority over difficult problems.

Yet these same ministers incessantly demand that the people of their congregations should contribute money for the construction of their churches, and there is inevitable trouble if they don't contribute. So the vicious cycle continues. When a church plans a project, the people must provide the necessary finances for the project. We find this picture of contradiction in Korean churches. Korean churches have been condemning money and calling it a seedbed of sin, forgetting that the "love of money" is the root of all evil, while cults spring up like mushrooms after a rain and delude believers by preposterous claims. Of course, these ministers also pray for the blessing of God on their sermons. And they pray for their people, including the blessing in material goods. Yet, because they do not teach clearly the basis on which Christians should and can prosper, Christians are confused. In order to prosper we must understand what the Word of God says regarding prosperity and then teach the truth clearly and systematically.

The first idea we should correct is the theory that poverty, pain, trial and tribulation are the ingredients of Christian virtue. Nowhere in the Bible is it written that meager meals and poor living conditions are pleasing to God. This does happen to some believers at times, but at such times they are learning to expand their faith and with spiritual growth will understand God's blessing of prosperity. Believers should note that God speaks much about "blessing" throughout the Old and New Testaments. They should allow these truths to be made alive by the Holy Spirit in their hearts. Unless God has a special plan for us, He wants us to live in comfort, with our needs met. Often, if God has instructed some people to live by faith, He has singled them out for a divine purpose or ministry. God is teaching them how to trust Him in difficult circumstances and how to discipline themselves to believe God for their needs. Not everyone is required to go through severe testing such as Paul endured, since they were not called to do a great work like Paul's in his generation.

Second, we must give up the idea that the material world is only for the devil. If the material world were only for the devil, what place should God possess—the God who created the heavens and the earth? It is certain that the material world passed into the hands of the devil after the fall of Adam and Eve. But now the material world has been restored to us through the death of Jesus Christ on the cross. His resurrection makes it even more certain.

Third, we must lay aside the thinking that spiritual blessings and heaven are all we need, and that material blessings are out of place for us. The salvation which Jesus wrought for us has the same power in the material world as the spiritual world. Yes, let us not confuse prosperity with greed! Greed is characteristic of the devil, while prosperity is an attribute of God. The prosperity God wants to see in our lives applies to the whole picture of living: child-rearing, our jobs, businesses, human relationships, the necessities of life, the stability of life, joy and so on.

Consequently, if we are made whole in our spirits, souls and bodies, the natural outcome is that we should prosper in every area of our lives. Jesus shed His precious blood and made out a deed—a certificate of title— calling for our prosperity in all things. The remaining work for us now is to exercise the rights and privileges that have already been given to us in order to obtain those provisions.

In spite of this, I think many people are not quite persuaded that Christians should prosper and that their whole lives should be blessed, including their material lives. For the sake of such Christians I will consider how God first created the material world and gave it to man as a gift.

God Created the Material World First

The Bible tells us clearly what attitude God took toward man's daily life and material blessings. God created the material world first, before He made man. He created light, the heavens, the earth, the sun, the moon and the stars. He made the trees, the herbs, the cattle and all other animals on the earth, the fish in the seas and streams, and the birds in the air. After God had finished creating the material universe for man, and everything was ready for him, then God made man in His own image on the last day. There remained no work for man to do when he was created. God did not leave anything which required man's help: "Thus the heavens and the earth were finished, and all the host of them. And on the seventh day God ended his work which he had made; and he rested on the seventh day from all his work which he had made" (Gen. 2:1-2).

The day after man was created was the Sabbath. Man had no work to do. He only had to enter God's rest, to enjoy and govern the beautiful material world God had created for him. Think about that! God prepared the "material" world first, because He knew that man needed it. It was our good God Himself who made the garden of Eden for Adam and Eve. In the midst of the garden, God placed all kinds of fruit-bearing trees, trees that were pleasant to look at and good for food. He instructed Adam and Eve to dress and care for the garden and enjoy its blessings. These trees set Adam and Eve completely free from care and worry about

55

obtaining the necessities of life. Our God is a generous God!

"And a river went out of Eden to water the garden; and from thence it was parted" (Gen. 2:10). This river was a fountainhead of life, assuring an endless flow of prosperity for the perfect man He had made. Rich, fertile land has always existed along rivers, producing abundance of fruit. Where rivers flowed, great civilizations always flourished.

God prepared abundant treasures in the garden of Eden. Pison, one of the four rivers flowing out of Eden, compassed the land of Havilah, where pure gold, bdellium and onyx were found. Along with the trees which provided the necessities of life, the river of life also yielded rich treasures in the garden which God had prepared for Adam and Eve. Man lacked nothing!

There was no need for Adam and Eve to sweat in hard labor. Today, sweat symbolizes the curse. The Bible states that the reason man had to sweat in his labor was that Adam disobeyed the commandment of God. As a result of his disobedience, he was banished from the garden of Eden. People today have to sweat for a living because they are all under the same curse as Adam. When man was living in the garden of Eden in the blessing of God, he was not created to sweat for his living. The sweat of society, caused by business problems, childhood problems, sickness and death, and the cultivation of the land which is covered with thorns and thistles, is all caused by the sin of Adam, resulting in the curse.

The world which God created first was a world where everything was provided for man and where one could prosper. It was a world where there was rich material wealth as well as things which could fully meet the needs of daily life. When God created human beings, He made us to live in close harmony with the material world. The relationship between natural substance and human beings is just like the relationship between blood and life. As life cannot exist without blood, so man cannot live without material things. Once we are born into this world, we can by no means escape the entanglement of economic life. Feeding, clothing and sheltering a family are problems concerned with material things. The workplace also belongs to that realm.

We must have an accurate understanding of the material world. God certainly created the material world for us in the beginning, and He originally planned that there would be no occasion for us to sweat in laborious toil. God wanted us to live an abundant life, prospering in all things. The material world was not originally possessed by the devil. But since today's world is under the power of the devil, no one except born-again Christians who obey God's Word can escape from the condition which brought man under the curse and made everything go wrong. Everyone screams that he is trapped in a corner, living in the environment which has been cursed and turned over to Satan. What is the outcome of the fall of Adam? In order to obtain changed circumstances in which we can prosper, it may be profitable to scrutinize our present state.

Why We Cannot Prosper

The Tree of Knowledge and the Sovereignty of God

The original happy state of man was destroyed and the garden of Eden became disordered because of human disobedience to God. Therefore, if we try to explain the present material life in the light of economic trends and social circumstances, our explanation will be incomplete. We Christians should first scrutinize ourselves to know whether there may be something wrong in our relationship with God, since our Lord does not change. He is *Jehovah-jirah*, who provides all our needs. God, who prepared everything for man in advance, gave the beautiful garden of Eden to Adam and Eve. The location was neither too cold nor too hot, nor was there any harm. He gave them the authority to rule over the garden. But He commanded them not to taste the fruit of the tree of knowledge in the middle of the garden. God strictly warned them that if they did they would die.

What does the fruit of the tree of knowledge signify? Why did God command that all other fruit might be eaten except the fruit of the tree of knowledge? If it was really true that one would die if he tasted the fruit of that particular tree, why did God plant such a dangerous tree?

The fruit of the tree of knowledge symbolizes the sovereign power of God the creator. The tree was planted to teach man the fact that because God is the creator and man the creature, man must submit himself to the authority of God and be obedient. When God commanded man not to eat of the fruit of the tree of knowledge, He did not tell him the reason why he should not eat. The almighty God does not have to explain. He only commands. Jesus didn't explain Himself before Caiaphas and Pontius Pilate when He was being tried before His crucifixion. He was the supreme being. He didn't have to explain. Making explanations and propounding theories are not actions appropriate to one who has authority. Therefore God did not explain to Adam and Eve why they should not eat of the fruit of the tree of knowledge. He simply told them, "Thou shalt not eat of it (the tree of knowledge): for in the day that thou eatest thereof thou shalt surely die'' (Gen. 2:17).

The fruit of the tree of knowledge was the only thing that God forbade Adam to eat. It represented the sovereignty of the creator, which could by no means be challenged by any creature. God gave all other things to Adam, but He would not allow him to infringe on His sovereignty. Consequently, it was predestined that there should be the tree of knowledge in the garden of Eden. God clearly proclaimed that He had sovereign power in the material world. Whenever Adam and Eve saw the fruit of the tree of knowledge, they thought, This signifies God's sovereignty. They were thus reminded of the necessity not to eat that fruit, because it symbolized God's sovereignty. Thus they would enjoy all the beauty and material wealth that God had given them. When Adam and Eve were obedient to the sovereignty of God, on that basis they were able to rule over the garden which God had prepared and to enjoy their privileges.

But one day Satan came to visit. Satan challenged the authority of God from the beginning. Satan proposed a different idea, questioning the rightness of God's commandment: "Yea, hath God said, Ye shall not eat of every tree that is in the garden?" (Gen. 3:1).

The question insinuated that God's decree might not be true. It was Satan's deceitful tactic to make the absolute decree of the supreme being into a relative one. Then Eve, whose interest was aroused by the insinuation of the devil, said, "We may eat of the fruit of the trees of the garden: but of the fruit of the tree which is in the midst of the garden, God hath said, Ye shall not eat of it, neither shall ye touch it, lest ye die" (Gen. 3:2-3).

The absolute decree of God, "Thou shalt surely die," was replaced by the relative worry, "Lest ye die." Once doubt came into the heart of Eve, and the commandment of God sounded relative, then Satan consolidated his power in her heart: "Ye shall not surely die" (Gen. 3:4).

God's commandment became relative and Satan's opinion became absolute. Satan immediately explained the reason for his opinion: "For God doth know that in the day ye eat thereof, then your eyes shall be opened, and ye shall be as gods, knowing good and evil" (Gen. 3:5).

The lesson we can learn from this is that God gives an absolute commandment which needs neither a reason nor an explanation, but Satan always tempts us by presenting a theory. So when you hear a theory which questions the authority of God, it is from Satan. When unbelief came into Eve's confession of faith, Satan confirmed it by saying, "Ye shall not die." As a result, Eve ate of the forbidden fruit and gave some to her husband.

Then man started on his life of infringing on the sovereign realm of God. The original theocratic world was replaced by a man-centered world. Man placed himself on the same level with God and began to discuss what was right and what was wrong, what was good and what was evil. Man turned away from his proper stance of acknowledging and obeying the sovereign will of God. Instead, he pushed himself forward to a position of equality with God. Man raised the argument that he would keep the commandments of God insofar as they were acceptable to him. If they weren't acceptable, he would not keep them. *Man* decided that *he* could either obey or not, and either believe or not. As a result, man lives a life which is contrary to God. He tries to judge between good and evil on the basis of human knowledge and wisdom.

The cosmic order of creation became confused and God could no longer walk together with fallen man. Then God drove Adam and Eve out of the garden of Eden. In refusing to acknowledge God's sovereign authority over the material world, they lost their right to possess it. The good and prosperous environment of the garden was now exchanged for a cursed and unprosperous one outside the garden. Work became so laborious that they had to sweat as they toiled. Sweat now became the norm of life.

God Never Allows His Sovereign Authority to Be Infringed Upon

As soon as Adam and Eve went astray from the path of obedience and submission to the will of God, trying to argue with God, putting themselves on the same level with God, He drove them out and away from the garden of Eden. He cursed the earth and made it bring forth thorns and thistles: "And unto Adam and Eve he said, Because thou hast hearkened unto the voice of thy wife, and hast eaten of the tree, of which I commanded thee, saying, Thou shalt not eat of it: cursed is the ground for thy sake; in sorrow shalt thou eat of it all the days of thy life; thorns and thistles shall it bring forth to thee; and thou shalt eat the herb of the field: In the sweat of thy face shalt thou eat bread, till thou return unto the ground; for out of it wast thou taken: for dust thou art, and unto dust shalt thou return" (Gen. 3:17-19).

How did this lost paradise happen? Man challenged the authority of God. God does not make much of the occasional doubts which His faithful children harbor. Though they disobey from time to time, He does not destroy them. Yet He never allows them to challenge His authority. How much God thinks of His divine authority is written in Romans 13:1-2: "Let every soul be subject unto the higher powers. For there is no power but of God: the powers that be are ordained of God. Whosoever therefore resisteth the power, resisteth the ordinance of God: and they that resist shall receive to themselves damnation.''

God never tolerates an argument against His sovereign authority. We can find examples of this in many places in the Bible. God anointed Saul to be king and gave him authority to rule. God gave him a special task: ''Now go and smite Amalek, and utterly destroy all that they have, and spare them not; but slay both man and woman, infant and suckling, ox and sheep, camel and ass'' (1 Sam. 15:3).

This was an order from God. God did not explain the reason and the conditions for this commandment when He gave it. But Saul raised an argument against the orders God had given. In disobedience he infringed on the sovereign authority of God, for in spite of the command of God that both man and woman should be utterly destroyed, Saul took Agag, the king of the Amalekites, alive. He violated the commandment that the oxen and sheep, camels and asses, should be destroyed. The written record tells us that he spared the best of the sheep and oxen and brought them back with him. When Samuel asked him why he committed such a sin, he tried to defend himself with what seemed to be a plausible excuse: ''But the people took of the spoil, sheep and oxen, the chief of the things which should have been utterly destroyed, to sacrifice unto the Lord thy God in Gilgal'' (1 Sam. 15:21).

Then Samuel rebuked the disobedience and arrogance of King Saul: ''When thou wast little in thine own sight, wast thou not made the head of the tribes of Israel, and the Lord anointed thee king over Israel?'' (1 Sam. 15:17). ''Hath the Lord as great delight in burnt offerings and sacrifices, as in obeying the voice of the Lord? Behold, to obey is better than sacrifice, and to hearken than the fat of rams. For rebellion is as the sin of witchcraft, and stubbornness is as iniquity and idolatry. Because thou hast rejected the word of the Lord, he hath also rejected thee from being king'' (1 Sam. 15:22-23).

Of course, King Saul did not intentionally violate the word of God. In his own heart, King Saul acted on what he thought was best—that he should spare the best and fattest of the cattle and sheep for sacrifice to God. This might have seemed natural from a human point of view. But King Saul infringed on the sovereign authority of God with his human wisdom.

Saul knew that all those cattle should be utterly destroyed. Despite the fact that he clearly understood God's commandment, he put his opinion of right and wrong before God's orders and insinuated that his ideas and opinions were better than God's word. This was as the "sin of witchcraft... and idolatry." Therefore God rejected King Saul without hesitation.

God will never tolerate a challenge against His sovereign authority. The archangel who challenged the authority of God was banished from heaven and became Satan. Adam and Eve were driven out of the garden of Eden. King Saul was driven away from his throne.

When King Uzziah infringed on the sovereignty of God, usurping the authority of the high priest, leprosy appeared on his forehead and he had to be confined to his house for the remainder of his life.

Jonah raised an argument with God when he was commanded to go to Nineveh. When he tried to go in the other direction, he suffered bitterly in the belly of a great fish.

Ananias and Sapphira died in an instant because of their sin of infringing on the sovereignty of God by lying to the Holy Spirit.

On the final day of this world, Satan will be judged for continuously challenging the sovereign authority of God since the time of creation. He will be cast into the lake of fire and brimstone to be burned there forever.

In Korea today we have leaders of cults who have violated the sovereign authority of God. They lift up their hearts, putting themselves in the place of God and calling themselves Messiah. In pride and self-conceit, they erect monuments to their own names, but God will destroy them because that is a grave infringement on His sovereignty.

The communists encroach on the world, and they too will be cursed because of their rebellion against the supreme authority of God. For they are not simply atheists, they are children of Satan; and they have seriously infringed on the sovereignty of God. The most thoroughgoing atheist in our world's history was Nietzsche. He said that God was dead and His body stank. He infringed on the supreme authority of God. As a result he died raving. Whoever challenges the sovereign authority of God is not forgiven but is removed from the world which God made.

How are we affected today by the curse of Adam? What relationship does that curse have to us? Let us consider this question.

The Image of Failure

In the parable of the prodigal son in Luke 15, we can see the image of Adam's fallen descendants who failed in everything. The second son demanded his right to his portion of his father's fortune and claimed it. This son's behavior is similar to the story of Adam and Eve when they asserted their freedom and independence from God and ate the forbidden fruit. The prodigal son thought that if he possessed money he would be happy and everything would be ideal. So he left his home with his part of the fortune, like Adam and Eve when they were driven out of the garden of Eden. Though it seemed for a while that a vast new world was welcoming him, what actually waited for him was the world now under the curse. What were the events?

First he said, "Give me the portion of goods that falleth to me." This shows that he had a wrong idea, that possession of wealth would bring him happiness. Today a lot of people seek happiness in the possession of wealth, like the prodigal son. People who have already challenged the sovereign authority of God and have rebelled against God can possess wealth, but they cannot possess happiness.

Howard Hughes and Jean Paul Getty, two of the richest men in the United States, died some years ago and left us with an important lesson. Howard Hughes left a fortune of $2 billion, but he was one of the most unhappy, lonely men in the world during the last ten years of his life. He shut himself in his room and led a solitary life, avoiding any contact with people because of anxiety and fear. When he died there was no one to mourn his death, no wife or children. Throughout his life he wandered, seeking pleasure with women with his hoard of money, but Hughes never found happiness.

Jean Paul Getty also possessed an astronomical fortune of almost $4 billion, but his private life was unhappy. He married five times and divorced all his wives. His oldest son died an alcoholic one year before Getty died. His life was just as unhappy as that of Hughes. The lives of these two striking figures show that when man fails to acknowledge the supreme God, his wealth and riches only cause more loneliness and anxiety. Those today who suffer most from insomnia because of anxiety and fear are those people who have wealth but no faith.

The prodigal son thought that if he found freedom in a far country, happiness would come to him. But he went to a far country without any purpose except to be free from responsibility. Freedom without a goal and responsibility is license, and it will bind rather than free us. License is always followed by emptiness. When emptiness surges up inside, we become desperate and reckless in the effort to regain the meaning of life. It is at such moments that horrible crimes are committed.

Today a lot of young people are running away from home thinking that if they are out of the sight of their parents, they will find the world of freedom they need, without restraint and responsibility. They feel that they will find their future. But seeking freedom beyond the boundaries of responsibility and duty breeds license and becomes the breeding place of evil. Freedom that is not according to the will of God leads to unhappiness. Today we see the fallen descendants of Adam and Eve banished from the garden of Eden, floundering in this unhappy state.

The prodigal son had the idea that if he sought pleasure "with riotous living," happiness would be his, but that pleasure quickly made him feel like one of the hogs. The Roman Empire declined in spite of her splendid civilization, as the result of moral laxity and the pursuit of pleasure. Today, a large number of people seek moments of pleasure in sex, alcohol and drugs, but all they get for their efforts is extreme emotional instability and a state of stupor.

The desire for this kind of pleasure is the result of lust. "Then when lust hath conceived, it bringeth forth sin; and sin, when it is finished, bringeth forth death" (James 1:15). Of course, joy is different from pleasure. We can have indescribable joy and peace in Jesus Christ, but we cannot derive joy from pleasure.

If we look at the United States or the Scandinavian countries of Western Europe, which have the most developed civilization today, we see sexual promiscuity caused by the blind pursuit of pleasure. Promiscuity has now reached an all-time high, and it has resulted in a rapidly increased rate of suicide, ever-intensifying crime rate, and fragmented and broken homes. This is the grim reality of life for Adam's descendants, who infringed on the sovereign power of God and departed from the joy of God.

Some people seek happiness in the possession of power, but that does not last either. Not only is power temporary, it causes one's enemies to increase. So the result of power is often a life of anxiety.

The last days of those two great conquerors, Alexander the Great and Napoleon, were miserable. Alexander the Great, who ascended the throne at the age of twenty, conquered all of Greece in less than ten years and took Syria and Egypt. He occupied countries all the way to India where it is said that he wept, for he had no more lands to conquer. He died at the age of only 33. Napoleon, who was dictator over all of Europe at one time, we condemned as a criminal and sent into exile.

The possession of power does not ensure happiness. Because of their sin, Adam and Eve were banished from the blessings which God had prepared for them, and all mankind has been born in sin because of their sin. Bible prophecy foretells: "This know also, that in the last days perilous times shall come. For men shall be lovers of their own selves, covetous, boasters, proud, blasphemers, disobedient to parents, unthankful, unholy, without natural affection, trucebreakers, false accusers, incontinent, fierce, despisers of those that are good, traitors, heady, highminded, lovers of pleasures more than lovers of God; having a form of godliness, but denying the power thereof: from such turn away" (2 Tim. 3:1-5).

Ever since Adam was banished for his disobedience, man has lived miserably, like the prodigal son who couldn't find satisfaction in anything: not from the possession of great wealth, nor from licentious indulgence in pleasure, nor from the power to command the world in which he lived.

The state in which everything goes wrong does not end in the life of an individual. The world is now stricken with severe famine. Every year tens of thousands of people die of hunger in the countries around the equator. It is reported that the population of the world increases by 200,000 people daily and 75 million people annually. World population will reach seven billion people by the year 2000 and will be 20 billion by 2050. In order to meet the needs of this population, 30 million tons of increased food supply must be produced annually. Today our world is reported to have a food surplus for only 27 days.

Nuclear weapons, stockpiled by the superpowers today, threaten a gloomy future of nuclear war. Not only nuclear weapons, but such dreadful weapons as germ bombs, gas bombs and neutron bombs are being produced competitively. When war broke out in Indochina, in the Middle East and in Africa, people trembled in fear over the possible annihilation which the war might bring about. In addition, the earth we occupy is being changed into an enormous garbage dump due to the pollution which is the by-product of mass production and mass consumption. The air is polluted and the rivers stink. Such mass production also drains the earth of its natural resources.

Besides that, however, there is one thing which is more terrible than the mess we are facing in our physical world. It is the spiritual famine, spiritual pollution and spiritual conflict. Hail Brunner, the American theologian and professor of economics, said in his book entitled *Diagnosing the Future of Mankind*, "World War I and the Great Depression struck a fatal blow to the legacy of the Victorian Era and the confidence based on faith in progress. Today's energy crisis warns us of the limitations of industry. On top of that is added the anxiety of civilization which is caused by overemphasis on material progress such as high income, quality food, miraculous advances in medical science, and the triumph of applied physics and chemistry, which does not satisfy the spiritual need of human beings. The last decade has been marked by darkness, cruelty and disorder. Can we expect a brighter future? The answer is 'No.' Will the future become darker than the past? The answer is 'Yes.' "

Professor Brunner further criticizes the highly industrialized and sophisticated American society: "During the last decade, American society has witnessed too many incidents which were discouraging: the Vietnam War, crime and violence, racial riots, bombing, hijacking of airplanes, and appalling terrorism. Violence and brutality on television, which is denounced by the American middle class, expose the unrest concealed beneath the surface of the seemingly comfortable American lifestyle. The present generation has failed to give their cherished values to their children because of marijuana, promiscuity, and other efforts which protest against tradition, particularly the school drop-outs among the children of the upper middle class. All these things bring us great anxiety."

At the 1973 conference of the Pan American Catholic Educators' Council, Dr. Victor Frankel, the famous Viennese psychiatrist, said this concerning the crisis of existential emptiness and meaninglessness: "A sense of meaninglessness is now covering the whole world like a flood, causing a morbid complex of so-called existential emptiness. Today, people have the implements of life and have money and power, too. Nevertheless they are miserable and unhappy. They still reach out their hands for narcotics or resort to suicide because they cannot achieve the goals of their lives even with the wealth and power they possess, as all of you well know. People throughout the world are thirsty for meaning in their lives, but since they cannot find it, they do not understand the meaning. The meaning of life is not invented. If we continue teaching our children that human beings are merely organisms of biological tissues or computers, it is only natural that they will be induced to use narcotics or resort to suicide when they grow up."

Is the world foreordained to roll in the wrong direction, thereby making everything go amiss? Are we bound for eternal destruction? No, we are not. God has delivered us from emptiness, meaninglessness, poverty and disease by sending us His only Son, Jesus Christ, to redeem man and bring him back into fellowship with God who gives us the meaning of life. Everything will go well with us and we will abundantly enjoy the blessings which God has prepared for us when we return to Him.

The prodigal son neither realized his cursed state nor thought of his father's house until he became hungry: "And when he came to himself, he said, How many hired servants of my father's have bread enough and to spare, and I perish with hunger! I will arise and go to my father, and I will say unto him, Father, I have sinned against heaven, and before thee, and am no more worthy to be called thy son: make me as one of thy hired servants" (Luke 15:17-19).

The prodigal son headed for his father's house with a repentant heart. Like the prodigal, our circumstances and living conditions are all affected when we are out of God's grace. The prodigal son was out of his father's grace in all his thinking, speech and behavior. The only hope remaining for him was the kindness and mercy of his father. So the prodigal son arose and drew near to the village where he was born. The Scripture says, "But when he was yet a great way off, his father saw him, and had compassion, and ran, and fell on his neck, and kissed him" (Luke 15:20).

His father, who had been at the entrance of the village each day, waiting and hoping that his son would return, was filled with indescribable joy. The father ordered his servants to put the best robe on him, to put a ring on his hand and shoes on his feet, and to kill the fatted calf for a feast. His father rejoiced with great forgiveness and a celebration that his son had returned home. The son had not expected such a lavishly prepared feast. But the son realized the true meaning of life was found in being under his father's love and care. Your true deliverance from emptiness, meaninglessness, poverty and disease is found in the heavenly Father's love and care also. In this parable, the prodigal son signifies fallen man, and the father represents God. When we come to God, saying, "Father, forgive me," He forgives and redeems us from the curse with His abounding grace and leads us to the present-day garden of Eden.

Does God pardon and forgive us without putting any conditions on us? No, He does not. There must be conditions, but the conditions are bearable. Since man was exiled from the garden to new surroundings where thorns and thistles grow, no one has ever been able to escape the thorns and thistles. In order to set us free from the thorns and thistles of failure and transfer us to the state of success, there had to be a mediator who could bring about this change. That mediator was Jesus Christ.

How can we ascertain that Jesus has delivered us from the curse? Of course we know that our spirits have been brought into good order by the death and resurrection of Jesus. How can we know that the death and resurrection of Jesus affects our daily lives as well? Let us find the answers to these questions.

The Cross and the Redemption of Circumstances

Adam was driven away from the presence of God and was cursed because he raised an argument against God, but Jesus Christ glorified God and redeemed us from that original sin through his total obedience to God. Jesus Christ was the only One who lived a sinless life on this earth. He did not raise an argument against the commandments of God, nor make excuses. Jesus was wholly obedient to the will of God, to the very death. Jesus said: "For I have not spoken of myself; but the Father which sent me, he gave me a commandment, what I should say, and what I should speak. And I know that his commandment is life everlasting" (John 12:49-50). "O, my Father, if it is possible, let this cup pass from me: nevertheless, not as I will, but as thou wilt" (Matt. 26:39). "Now is my soul troubled; and what shall I say? Father, save me from this hour: but for this cause came I unto this hour. Father, glorify thy name" (John 12:27-28).

In agreement with His Father, that His death on the cross was the will of God, Jesus did not consider the pain and separation but willingly laid down His life in obedience to God. It is written in Philippians 2:8: "He humbled himself, and became obedient unto death, even the death of the cross."

Adam had been cursed with exile because he exalted himself. Jesus atoned for that curse, setting us free from the bondage of death through His obedience. Should anyone still be in prison after being pardoned? Jesus not only pardoned our sins and saved us, but delivered us from the "prison," the punishment of sin. What was that punishment? It was the curse of the thorns and thistles: the state of being a failure in all things. From these thorns and thistles—the curse of being a failure—we have been set free!

"Christ hath redeemed us from the curse of the law, being made a curse for us: for it is written, Cursed is everyone that hangeth on a tree" (Gal. 3:13). Rejoice! You have been set free from the curse. Now we must carefully examine whether Jesus redeemed our environment when He was crucified.

The Poverty of Jesus and Our Prosperity

"For ye know the grace of our Lord Jesus Christ, that, though He was rich, yet for your sakes he became poor, that ye through his poverty might be rich" (2 Cor. 8:9). The meaning of this scripture is obvious.

As we know, Jesus was very rich. Though He was God and He was the creator, and He possessed all heaven and earth and everything in them, He gave up all His wealth. He was conceived as a baby, born in a humble manger in Bethlehem and lived as a poor man during His life on earth. The Bible says, "And Jesus saith unto him, The foxes have holes, the birds of the air have nests; but the Son of man hath not where to lay his head" (Matt. 8:20).

Why would the creator-God, who made everything by the word of His mouth, go around so poor on the earth that He would have no place to lay His head? Why did Jesus, who fed more than 5,000 people and had food left over, lead such a destitute life that He looked for fruit on a fig tree? We know that He was often out all night, exposed to the dew of heaven. He often slept on the ground because He had no other place to sleep. Why did He do that? The Bible answers, "That ye through his poverty might be rich" (2 Cor. 8:9).

If we do not receive the "riches" as stated in this scripture, we make the poverty of Jesus of no effect. We have an important responsibility: to receive the prosperous life, a life flowing with all the provision you and I will ever need—which He made possible for us by living in poverty. If we live a life of poverty without a special reason, as described earlier, we are insulting Jesus. Here the legitimate "special reason" could be that we volunteer to become poor by giving all we have to the work of God, or that under a great persecution we become poor to give glory to God. Other than these reasons, if we do not enjoy the prosperity provided for us by Jesus Christ, but we live in poverty, we bring shame to the name of Christ who became poor so that we might become rich.

Of course, the virtue of those who live in poverty without complaining and discouragement is commendable, but poverty in itself is never a thing which a man can be proud of, for it makes the poverty of Jesus void. So, if there is no special reason, encourage yourself in the Lord that His will is the fulfillment of your needs and your prosperity. Make up your mind that you will do your best to prosper, and God will help you. This is the way to glorify Christ scripturally.

Jesus Bore Our Curses

In the account of the crucifixion, we find the answer to the question, "How did Jesus redeem us from the punishment of sin?" That Jesus wore a crown of thorns as He was being led to the cross is very symbolic because thorns were a part of the curse after Adam was banished from the garden of Eden. It is very significant that as Jesus hung on the cross dying for you and me, a crown of thorns was placed on His head—the very symbol of the curse which had been placed on man. This shows that Jesus bore all the curse placed upon the human race because of the fall of Adam. Though it was Adam who committed the sin, it was Jesus who suffered the pain as He took the curse upon Himself. He canceled Adam's sin, and He restored man from failure and the curse to freedom from failure and the curse. No matter how good a plan we may follow in our work, if "thorns" stand in our way, we cannot do anything for ourselves. On the other hand, if the curse has been removed, blessing will come to every area of our lives. The cursed land will turn into good land flowing with milk and honey and God's blessings. Every area of our lives will be redeemed to live in newness of life.

The cross on which Jesus was nailed was also a symbol of the curse. We can be delivered from the punishment of the curse and sin through His crucifixion on the cross: "Christ hath redeemed us from the curse of the law, being made a curse for us: for it is written, Cursed is everyone that hangeth on a tree: that the blessing of Abraham might come on the Gentiles through Jesus Christ; that we might receive the promise of the Spirit through faith" (Gal. 3:13-14).

As this scripture indicates, Jesus was made a curse for us. He redeemed us from the curse of the law. What is the curse of the law? "But it shall come to pass, if thou wilt not hearken unto the voice of the Lord thy God, to observe to do all his commandments and his statutes which I command thee this day; that all these curses shall come upon thee, and overtake thee: Cursed shalt thou be in the city, and cursed shalt thou be in the field. Cursed shall be thy basket and thy store. Cursed shall be the fruit of thy body, and the fruit of thy land, the increase of thy kine, and the flocks of thy sheep. Cursed shalt thou be when thou comest in, and cursed shalt thou be when thou goest out" (Deut. 28:15-19).

How could anyone be more thoroughly cursed than that? It is written that we are cursed when we do not obey the Word of God. Adam and his descendants are of course under this curse until they come to Jesus and confess their sins.

By hanging on a cross prepared for people who were cursed, Jesus redeemed from the curse of the law all those who were grinding their teeth and sweating in the agony of their cursed circumstances. To redeem means to "bring back" one who has been sold as a slave by the payment of ransom. We became slaves to Satan through Adam's disobedience.

Power in the Name of Jesus Christ

After His ascension, Jesus shared the authority and power of His name with us that we might pray for all things. Jesus Christ! The name of Jesus has the only power for salvation and redemption from all curses and punishment. In order to be saved from sin and have a born-again experience, we call on His name: "Neither is there salvation in any other: for there is none other name under heaven given among men, whereby we must be saved" (Acts 4:12).

The power of Jesus' name is manifested when our sins are forgiven. Our sins are forgiven through that power, as it is written: "To him give all the prophets witness, that through his name whosoever believeth in him shall receive remission of sins" (Acts 10:43).

The name of Jesus Christ is needed for receiving the baptism of the Holy Spirit: "Repent, and be baptized everyone of you in the name of Jesus Christ for the remission of sins, and ye shall receive the gift of the Holy Ghost" (Acts 2:38).

His name is also used for the healing of our bodies. "They shall lay hands on the sick, and they shall recover" (Mark 16:18).

And when we pray for everything we need in our lives, as it is written, "If ye shall ask anything in my name, I will do it" (John 14:14). "Whatsoever ye shall ask the Father in my name, he will give it you" (John 16:23).

Jesus said that He would send the Holy Spirit to help us. The name of Jesus Christ becomes the guarantee of our rights. We can use that name without hesitation for success in everything. When we pray for prosperity in the name of Jesus, the Holy Spirit removes the thorns for us. Therefore, when we use the name of Jesus Christ, it means that we use the highest power there is in heaven or on earth.

Results of Redemption

Why did Jesus redeem us at such a terrible cost, wearing the crown of thorns, enduring the agony of being nailed to the cross and being pierced with a spear? "That the blessing of Abraham might come on the Gentiles through Jesus Christ; that we might receive the promise of the Spirit through faith" (Gal. 3:14).

Jesus Christ paid our debt for sin that He might bless us with the blessings of Abraham. What are the blessings of Abraham? He was a man who was counted to be righteous because of his great faith. By faith he left his hometown in obedience to God's promise. Therefore, the blessings of Abraham are first of all to be made righteous by faith and receive salvation. In addition, Abraham was the fountainhead of blessings:

"And I will make of thee a great nation, and I will bless thee, and make thy name great; and thou shalt be a blessing: and I will bless them that bless thee, and curse him that curseth thee: and in thee shall all the families of the earth be blessed" (Gen. 12:2-3). Besides the blessings of children, material wealth and long life, the blessings of Abraham become the source of blessing others as well. If we are blessed with the blessings of Abraham, though we may go through many trials and tribulations like Abraham, we can live a life which lacks nothing.

We have examined how the cross of Jesus Christ redeemed us from the punishment of poverty and the curse. Jesus not only forgave us our sins, but He also redeemed us from these punishments for sin. Now we can ask God for blessings and receive them. In order to do that, we must prepare our hearts.

The Way to an Ever-prosperous Life

We are redeemed and delivered from the curse which has always followed us, like the punishment which Adam received. Satan can no longer come to intimidate us with false accusations. We do not have to live in fear and anxiety as we did in the past, nor with timidity as a debtor. No one is imposing the punishment of sin upon us. We are not pointed at with scorn because we are sons of Adam. So hold up your head, lift up your eyes and look up to heaven! Can't you see your name written there as a son of God?

We are the people for whom everything should go well. The only thing left is that we must erase our old self-image by which we have always perceived ourselves in the negative lights of being oppressed, robbed and unworthy, as the punishment for our sin. Now we must adopt the new self-image in its place. Now we can boldly cry, "I was made by God and I am His child: I have become a new creature by the blood of Jesus Christ; I owe no man anything—only to love my brother as myself. I have been redeemed from the punishment of sin because Jesus wore the crown of thorns.

Some people still ask, "What more should we do to enjoy God's blessings? Hasn't our destination already been changed by the crucifixion of Jesus Christ?"

Though delicacies from all the world would be spread on a table, they would be meaningless to us unless we tasted and enjoyed them. Though we had rain at the end of a drought season, we could never fill an empty rain barrel unless we took the lid off. Likewise, however well the blessings

71

of God may have been ordained and prepared and extended to us, we can never partake until we receive them. Then we will enjoy them with thanksgiving.

Our daily work has very important meaning in the sense that it becomes an essential condition. With it we cannot enter into our blessings for all things, though it may be as simple as eating with a spoon or opening the lid of a rain barrel to catch rain water.

Let's look into the details, one by one, of the conditions for our work.

God's Sovereign Authority and the Tithe

The irrevocable offense in Adam's life was his infringement upon God's sovereign authority. Adam could not be allowed to eat of the tree of life and live forever, for a curse necessarily follows the one who infringes on the sovereignty of God. Accordingly, Adam was cursed and banished from the garden of Eden and was destined to walk in the path of affliction where thorns and thistles grew.

The Tree of Knowledge in the Present Time

You will probably think, The tree of knowledge was in the garden of Eden, but it doesn't exist in today's world, does it? But the tree of knowledge (actually representing God's sovereign authority) is even more clearly before our eyes today.

Although the tree of knowledge that was in the garden of Eden may not exist today, its meaning is still before our eyes. In today's spiritual world, the sovereign authority of God is manifested through Jesus Christ. Therefore, when we accept Jesus Christ as our Savior and He is at the center of our lives, the faith that is in us is a manifestation of God's sovereign authority. But today there are some people who infringe upon the sovereign authority of God by either denying Jesus Christ or misunderstanding Him. False teaching on the redemption of Jesus Christ brings eternal destruction to those who teach it as well as to those who listen and follow it. Jesus Christ represents the sovereignty of God, and we must not violate His sovereignty or the wrath of God will come upon us. The apostle John said, "He that hath the Son hath life; and he that hath not the Son of God hath not life" (1 John 5:12).

If a man has no life, then he is dead. When Adam took the forbidden fruit and tasted it, death was pronounced on him.

Also, however spiritual someone may seem, if that person preaches things other than the doctrines of the Scriptures: that Jesus was born of a virgin, crucified for the redemption of the whole world, rose on the third day, ascended into heaven, sits at the right hand of God and is coming again—then such a person is a son of Satan and is under the judgment of wrath.

Any false idea about Jesus Christ is seed sown by the spirit of antichrist. Satan still tries to keep us from confessing Jesus Christ as Lord and Savior, and he deceives us into infringing upon the authority of God by eating the forbidden fruit. "Beloved, believe not every spirit, but try the spirits whether they are of God: because many false prophets are gone out into the world. Hereby know ye the Spirit of God: Every spirit that confesseth that Jesus Christ is come in the flesh is of God: and every spirit that confesseth not that Jesus Christ is come in the flesh is not of God: and this is that spirit of antichrist" (1 John 4:1-3).

In Malachi we can see that God cursed the Israelites for infringing upon God's sovereign authority in a way similar to Adam's infringement on that sovereignty: "Even from the days of your fathers ye are gone away from mine ordinances, and have not kept them. Return unto me, and I will return unto you, saith the Lord of hosts. But ye said, Wherein shall we return? Will a man rob God? Yet ye have robbed me. But ye say, Wherein have we robbed thee? In tithes and offerings. Ye are cursed with a curse, for ye have robbed me, even this whole nation" (Mal. 3:7-9).

Through this scripture we can know that the curse in the garden of Eden and the curse in Malachi were both incurred by infringing upon the sovereign authority of God. The curse in the garden of Eden came by stealing the fruit of the tree of knowledge, and the curse in Malachi came by stealing the tithe. Just as the tree of knowledge stood in the old days in the garden of Eden, so the tithe still stands as a symbol of God's sovereignty in today's material world.

Satan's Temptation Against Tithing

Through Satan's interference we are able to understand more clearly that the tithe is a "symbol" of God's sovereign authority. This is the first target of Satan's wicked maneuver. He tenaciously tempted Eve until she finally gave in and ate the fruit of the tree of knowledge. He incited Herod to attempt the murder of Jesus when He came into this world. Satan followed Jesus wherever He went and interfered with His work.

Today countless Christians find it difficult to give their tithe, in spite of their prayers and tears, because Satan sticks to them and obstructs them with temptations. Satan tempts us with enticing words like these: "Since tithing belongs to the old traditions of the Jewish law, it no longer binds us who live in the dispensation of grace. God knows you are poor, so it is all right for you to postpone paying this obligation until you can better afford it. Then you can compensate for this negligence by giving a double portion of your tithe.'' This is a typical argument that Satan uses to keep us from paying our tithe, and it leads us to a surer conviction that the tithe symbolizes the sovereignty of God. Is the devil's argument therefore valid? First, let us consider the argument that the tithe is a relic from the dispensation of the law.

The law was first given to the people of Israel through Moses, but the Bible tells us that Abraham, who lived 430 years before Moses, paid tithes: ''And Melchizedek king of Salem brought forth bread and wine: and he was the priest of the most high God. And he blessed him, and said, Blessed be Abram of the most high God, possessor of heaven and earth: and blessed be the most high God, which hath delivered thine enemies into thy hand. And he gave him tithes of all'' (Gen. 14:18-20).

The Bible tells us further that Jacob, the grandson of Abraham, was blessed in a dream in which angels were ascending and descending from God. He vowed that he would continue giving his tithe when he fled from home to his mother's brother to avoid the wrath of his older brother: ''And Jacob vowed a vow, saying, If God will be with me, and will keep me in this way that I go, and will give me bread to eat, and raiment to put on, so that I come again to my father's house in peace; then shall the Lord be my God: and this stone, which I have set for a pillar, shall be God's house: and of all that thou shalt give me I will surely give the tenth unto thee'' (Gen. 28:20-21).

During New Testament times, did Jesus say that we no longer need to give the tithe? In which place of the Bible is it written that we are no longer bound by the obligation of tithing because it is a relic of the dispensation of law, which should be abandoned? We must see that the argument that the obligation of tithing was binding only during the dispensation of the law is a temptation and a trick of Satan to violate God's sovereignty. God's commandment concerning the tithe is the word of the living God who is the same yesterday, today and forever.

Second, let us analyze the temptation that we may put this obligation off until we can financially better afford it. Since Satan ''cometh not but for to steal, and to kill and to destroy'' (John 10:10), his deliberate lie in this case clearly shows how false and abominable his argument is. Satan does not want us to prosper. Consequently, he knows that if we follow his advice in putting off paying our tithes, we will become increasingly poorer. There is no place in the Bible that says we should pay two-tenths of our income. God wants us to tithe in order to give us a prosperous life, by making us admit the fact that sovereignty over the material world belongs to God and that we must be obedient to Him.

It is by no means true that God is so poor that He needs our tithes. God is the creator of the universe, who made the heavens and the earth. He could create another world if He wanted to. In Psalm 50:9-12 we read: "I will take no bullock out of thy house, nor he goats out of thy flock: For every beast of the forest is mine, and the cattle upon a thousand hills. I know all the fowls of the mountains: and the wild beasts of the field are mine. If I were hungry, I would not tell thee: for the world is mine, and the fulness thereof."

Satan comes to us and accuses God. He distorted God's will in the garden of Eden by saying to Eve, "Ye shall not surely die: for God doth know that in the days ye eat thereof, then your eyes shall be opened, and ye shall be as gods, knowing good and evil" (Gen. 3:4-5).

Satan distorts God's image concerning tithing as if God takes away our money for His own needs. If we give in to the devil and think lightly of God's sovereignty by stealing the tithes, we shall live in an endless curse. We may never be so rich as to give two-tenths of our income. Even if we did, it would be very difficult. Though we may be poor and have little to give, we must still give a tenth back to God no matter what our situation may be. If we are poor, we must tithe so that we may become prosperous, for God's blessing is poured out upon us when we acknowledge His sovereignty in His tithing plan.

Tithing and the Blessing of Material Things

Tithing is a beautiful sacrifice. If we are obedient in this way our natural response will be to exercise our faith that God will bless us.

The meeting between Abram and Melchizedek which is recorded for us in Genesis may help us understand God's plan for tithing (see Genesis 14). King Chedorlaomer was like Hitler. He took over five cities and forced the people to pay tribute to him. Finally, they revolted and there was a battle in which King Chedorlaomer won. He also took Lot and his family as prisoners. Lot was Abram's nephew. When Abram heard the news, he went out with his 318 servants and attacked at night. Abram won a great victory and brought back Lot with his family and servants and all the goods. On his way home he met Melchizedek. Then Abram gave tithes to Melchizedek of all that he had gained in battle. "After these things the word of the Lord came unto Abram in a vision, saying, Fear not, Abram: I am thy shield, and thy exceeding great reward" (Gen. 15:1).

This was the blessing given to Abram, because he tithed. The Bible states that Abraham (as his name was changed) was not only the father of the Jews as pertaining to the flesh, but the father of all of them that believe, as pertaining to the faith. Today, those who have faith like that of Abraham receive the same blessings: "Know ye therefore that they which are of faith, the same are the children of Abraham. And the scripture, foreseeing that God would justify the heathen through faith, preached before the gospel unto Abraham, saying, In thee shall all nations be blessed. So then they which be of faith are blessed with faithful Abraham" (Gal. 3:7-8).

When we lived for the world, we were robbed of everything and became prisoners of the devil. Abraham went out and brought back all that was taken by King Chedorlaomer, who represents Satan in this passage of Scripture. Abram is here our type of Christ, and through faith in Christ we also have recovered all that we lost.

"For whatsoever is born of God overcometh the world: and this is the victory that overcometh the world, even our faith. Who is he that overcometh the world, but he that believeth that Jesus is the Son of God?" (1 John 5:4-5).

Melchizedek was a type of Jesus. In Hebrews 6:20 we read, "Whither the forerunner is for us entered, even Jesus, made an high priest forever after the order of Melchizedek."

When we believe in Jesus Christ, we become the victors who are translated from death, hell and the position of the devil's slaves, to life, heaven and the position of God's children, just as Abraham triumphed in the battle and recovered all that was taken away. We not only become victors, but we also become eligible to partake of the sacraments of holy communion. So when we pay our tithes, the same blessing that was given to Abraham comes to us.

There are a lot of Christians today who do not enjoy the blessings which are available to every Christian, because they do not tithe. When we pay our tithes to God, it becomes the expression of our faith in God's blessing.

What do the blessing and assurance which Abraham received from God mean to us? "I am thy shield, and thy exceeding great reward" (Gen. 15:1).

In biblical times a shield was used to protect the body in battle. While we live on this earth, our enemy, the devil, brings us temptation, tribulation, trouble, agony and sorrow time and again. But if we pay our tithes, God becomes our shield and makes us overcomers. If God is our shield and our shelter, we never need to worry. In Psalm 121:5-6 we read, "The Lord is thy keeper: the Lord is thy shade upon thy right hand. The sun shall not smite thee by day, nor the moon by night." Therefore we can boldly confess our faith: "Who shall separate us from the love of Christ? Shall tribulation, or distress, or persecution, or famine, or nakedness, or peril, or sword? Nay, in all these things we are more than conquerors through Him that loved us" (Rom. 8:35,37).

The second assurance of the promise which God gave to Abraham was "the exceeding great reward" (Gen. 15:1). Today the reward which the world pays is extremely futile. The wealth, glory and honor of the world are always fickle, and we will lose tomorrow what we gain today. "For all flesh is grass, and all the glory of man as the flower of the grass. The grass withereth, and the flower thereof falleth away" (1 Pet. 1:24).

The reward God promised to Abraham was not a reward which rusts or is eaten by cankerworms. The great Lord God who made heaven and earth has become our reward, and He pays the reward of abundance and prosperity: "If God be for us, who can be against us?" (Rom. 8:31). "I will never leave thee, nor forsake thee" (Heb. 13:5). "Lo, I am with you alway, even unto the end of the world" (Matt. 28:20).

If Abraham prospered by paying his tithes, modern believers should also receive the same blessings. "Bring ye all the tithes into the storehouse, that there may be meat in mine house, and prove me now herewith, saith the Lord of hosts, if I will not open you the windows of heaven, and pour you out a blessing, that there shall not be room enough to receive it. And I will rebuke the devourer for your sakes, and he shall not destroy the fruits of your ground; neither shall your vine cast her fruit before the time in the field, saith the Lord of hosts. And all nations shall call you blessed: for ye shall be a delightsome land, saith the Lord of hosts" (Mal. 3:10-12).

The blessing which will be poured out for us, due to tithing, cannot be written more certainly and correctly than this. This passage of Scripture is true, for God cannot lie.

When we pay our tithes to acknowledge the sovereignty of God, there are several things we must be careful about. First, we must give "all the tithes." We must give the precise amount: one-tenth of all our income. If we interpret the regulation of the tithe freely, as we like, and give thank offerings, Sunday offerings and alms out of the tithe, that is not paying all the tithe. We must keep our tithe intact. As for other offerings and alms, we can give them according to the guidance of the Holy Spirit.

It is written, "That there may be meat in mine house." We must give our tithes to the house where we get our spiritual meat, namely one's own church, for if we take the tithe and decide to give it to some other place or person, according to our whim, this is still not acknowledging the sovereignty of God as we read in Malachi 3:10-12.

God promised that He would give us two blessings if we keep these two conditions. One is the blessing to protect us from disaster. However large our income may be, if we encounter a succession of disasters, we may be in worse condition than if we had no income at all. The other is the blessing of inner strength. Though we make a lot of money, if illness and trouble strike us, our money disappears like "water poured down the drain." We still will not have what we hoped to have, because we did not pay all of our tithes.

So we see that paying tithes is an act by which we acknowledge the sovereignty of God and practice obedience. It is the key of faith with which we can open the door of blessings prepared for us by Jesus Christ. By accepting Jesus Christ as our Savior, we have acknowledged the spiritual sovereignty of God, and by giving our tithes we have admitted His supreme power over the material world. When we are obedient, it follows that God's blessings come to us and we prosper in all things.

The Law of Material Blessings

God often wants to give us a special blessing. This blessing is one with a purpose. Through paying our tithes our daily lives are blessed with plenty, but when God gives us a blessing of abundance for a special purpose, we can use the law of material blessings with faith.

We do not give our tithes so that we may receive blessings. We must pay our tithes as the sign that we acknowledge the sovereignty of God and are obedient to Him. If we accept God's plan of acknowledging His sovereignty through paying tithes, God makes our land beautiful and blesses it with fruit. But when we start a new thing with a special purpose, we must use the following laws that we may be blessed by God again.

The Law of Sowing and Reaping

When we start a new business under the guidance of the Holy Spirit, we can make the most of our faith according to the law of sowing and reaping. Faith is like a grain of mustard seed. Unsown faith gives us no profit; but when it is sown in the earth, it grows into a tree, and the birds may sit on its branches. "But this I say, He which soweth sparingly shall reap also sparingly; and he which soweth bountifully shall reap also bountifully. Every man according as he purposeth in his heart, so let him give; not grudgingly, or of necessity: for God loveth a cheerful giver. And God is able to make all grace abound toward you; that ye, always having all sufficiency in all things, may abound to every good work: (as it is written, He hath dispersed abroad; he hath given to the poor: his righteousness remaineth forever. Now he that ministereth seed to the sower both minister bread for your food, and multiply your seed sown, and increase the fruits of your righteousness)'' (2 Cor. 9:6-10).

What wonderful words these are! The seed of faith, unless it is sown cheerfully, profits us nothing, for at the very moment we offer our material, our faith is loosed. If only we could have such faith, the miracle which moves mountains would come to pass in our lives: ''And Jesus said unto them, Because of your unbelief: for verily I say unto you, if ye have faith as a grain of mustard seed, ye shall say unto this mountain, Remove hence to yonder place; and it shall remove; and nothing shall be impossible unto you'' (Matt. 17:20).

Jesus made no exaggerations. ''Nothing shall be impossible unto you'' is the word of promise which will come true if only we have faith as a grain of mustard seed. This faith was given to us when we acknowledged Jesus as our Savior. What is left now is the job of sowing: sowing with money, time and our bodies that the grain of mustard seed may bud and the stem grow. That is faith. We must not give grudgingly, nor only because it is necessary, but we should sow cheerfully as our hearts listen to God. Then He will bless us, and what is sown in obedience to His direction will bring forth abundance.

The Law of Investment

This signifies that we invest money for the work of God under the guidance of the Holy Spirit. Secular people invest and earn profits. Likewise, when Christians invest in the work of God, they can receive the profit of blessing which God prepares for them. The Bible says this clearly: ''Now ye Philippians know also, that in the beginning of the gospel, when I departed from Macedonia, no church communicated with me as concerning giving and receiving, but ye only. For even in Thessalonica ye sent once and again unto my necessity. Not because I desire a gift: but I desire fruit that may abound to your account. But I have all, and abound: I am full, having received of Epaphroditus the things which were sent from you, an odour of a sweet smell, a sacrifice acceptable, wellpleasing to God. But my God shall supply all your need according to His riches in glory by Christ Jesus'' (Phil. 4:15-19).

When we invest in the work of God, He will reward us with abundance.

This is the law of investment. If we invest in the work of God, He will return to us 30-fold, 60-fold and 100-fold.

The Bible tells a lot about the people who are blessed by using the law of investment. Among those examples are the widow woman of Zarephath and Andrew and the lad who gave the five loaves of bread and two fish. With the investment of "a handful of meal and a little oil," the widow experienced the miracle which saved her and her son from starvation. The meal and the oil were all that the widow had. For her, it made no difference whether she ate one more meal or not. She had exhausted all the possibilities to avoid starvation. In this circumstance she received a miraculous profit (1 Kings 17:8-16).

Peter invested his ship, time and effort in Jesus and received a shipload of fish. Jesus entered the ship of Simon Peter and taught the people. Simon was washing the nets and was tired, for he had worked all night and had taken nothing. Nevertheless, he pushed off a little from the shore in obedience to the words of Jesus and waited. After a while Jesus told him that he should launch out into the deep and let down his nets for a draught. In Peter's experience the words of Jesus were against common sense, for if you cast nets in the Sea of Galilee in the daytime, the water is so clear that the fish will see the net and will get away. Still, Peter invested in faith and as a result he caught so many fish that the nets broke. This was the dividend from his investment for God (Luke 5:1-11).

The boy with his lunch experienced the miracle which fed more than 5,000 men, not counting all the thousands of women and children. But twelve baskets of fragments were left over. Five small loaves of bread and two fish were all he invested in the work of God (Luke 9:11-17).

If we cheerfully participate as well as invest in the work of God, He will accept it as a savory offering and fill our needs abundantly. Our Lord owes us nothing. He does not want to owe anything to anyone. He wants us to love one another. When the Holy Spirit tells us to invest in souls, we should not hesitate. We should invest in the work of God and experience His giving the increase.

The Law of Echo

The third law by which we can receive a special blessing is explained by the law of echo. If we don't say anything when standing on a mountaintop, there is no answer, but if we shout, the echo comes back like an answer. Likewise, when we do something which gives glory to God, it will return to us with added blessing. Nothing is hid or lost from God. The Bible says, "Give, and it shall be given unto you; good measure, pressed down, and shaken together, and running over, shall men give into your bosom. For with the same measure that ye mete withal it shall be measured to you again'' (Luke 6:38).

God did not say He would just return what we had given Him. He said that He would give us good measure and that it would be so pressed down and shaken together that it would run over!

Dear brothers and sisters who read this book, do not give grudgingly. Give cheerfully as the Lord directs you to give. Give of your life to God and your neighbors. If we grab at material things or our time, those things will slip away from us; but increasing blessings will come to us when we give to others, like a rolling snowball gathers more snow.

A lot of people come to me and ask, ''Pastor, how can I be rich?'' I always teach them the law of echo. This is a simple law, but very hard to practice. In our generation, we find many examples of those who succeed by making good use of the law of echo.

The famous steel magnate, Andrew Carnegie, was a multi-millionaire, but when he immigrated to America from Scotland, he was like an orphan and didn't even finish elementary school. In spite of a succession of hardships, when he established his steel company, he knew a lot about the law of echo. His dream was to provide a lot of people with jobs and teach his employees to have their own bank accounts. His goal was to obtain wealth so that he could give it away. This was the law of echo in practice, and it eventually made him the steel magnate of the century.

Henry Ford, the pioneer of the modern auto industry, was also familiar with the law of echo. His goal was ''How can I make the best automobile for the cheapest price so it could be available to the most people?'' He dreamed of placing inexpensive wheels at the feet of the American people. His idea created waves and sent back echoes which eventually made him a millionaire.

This experience from the business world also illustrates a spiritual principle. If we want the blessings of God, we should first of all get free from the selfish life. If I give benefits to others and cause them to be blessed, the law of echo will cause the blessing to come back to me 30-fold, 60-fold and 100-fold. In this world, we can claim nothing as ours, but when we learn to help or bless others with what we have, the benefit will come back to us, becoming our own. This is the law of echo.

Thus far we have looked into the secret of prosperity. When we put this secret into practice, making it our rule to live by, the blessing of plenty and prosperity will be poured out for us like the water flowing from an open tap. Though abundant blessings are given to us through the good practice of this law, if we do not prepare a vessel to receive the blessings, we still cannot receive. This vessel is the heart. By showing the attitudes which lead to failure, we hope to help avoid pitfalls on the path to prosperity.

Attitudes of the Mind That Lead to Failure

"Keep thy heart with all diligence; for out of it are the issues of life" (Prov. 4:23).

The Lord God is our Father, the creator and the very root of our lives, the cause of our being and the source of all things.

"In the beginning was the Word, and the Word was with God, and the Word was God" (John 1:1).

"But the righteousness which is of faith speaketh on this wise, Say not in thine heart, Who shall ascend into heaven? (that is, to bring Christ down from above): or, Who shall descend into the deep? (that is, to bring Christ up from the dead). But what saith it? The word is nigh thee, even in thy mouth, and in thy heart: that is, the word of faith, which we preach; that if thou shalt confess with thy mouth the Lord Jesus, and shalt believe in thine heart that God hath raised him from the dead, thou shalt be saved" (Rom. 10:6-9).

God, the originator of our lives, dwells in our hearts through the Word. God is not the God of the Jews only, and He is not only the God of those who lived 2,000 years ago. He is not a remote deity who will have nothing to do with us until some future date. God is the God who dwells in our hearts right now, today, through the Holy Spirit! Each of us is the temple of God. The Bible reads: "Know ye not that ye are the temple of God, and that the Spirit of God dwelleth in you?" (1 Cor. 3:16).

We who have been washed by the blood of Jesus are not only chosen to be the children of Israel but have in our hearts the same Holy Spirit who was in the garden of Eden, lived in the tabernacle in the time of Moses and lived in Jesus Christ while here on earth. The place where God is, wherever that may be, is heaven. When God lives in our hearts, our hearts become heaven.

"The kingdom of God cometh not with observation: Neither shall they say, Lo here! or, lo there! for, behold, the kingdom of God is within you" (Luke 17:20-21).

Because the kingdom of God is in our hearts, we should enjoy the pleasure of heaven in our living, such as eating, drinking and wearing our clothes. That is the life of prosperity. In order that we may prosper, we must have God in our hearts. Then we will bear fruit: "I am the vine, ye are the branches: He that abideth in me, and I in him, the same bringeth forth much fruit: for without me ye can do nothing" (John 15:5).

Since our hearts are vessels, unless they are clean, the kingdom of God will not abide in us. Holiness and purity are the attributes of God. If we grieve the Holy Spirit by failure to keep our hearts pure, God will not dwell within us and we cannot bear the fruit of prosperity.

How can we know whether our hearts are pure or not? Our hearts are very difficult to be fathomed. An old Korean saying states, "It is hard to fathom the minds and intentions of men." How can we know whether our heart is pure or not? Our thoughts reflect our heart and they come out of our mouth wearing the clothes of speech. Therefore purity of our hearts can be measured from our speech.

It is written that God saw the world which He had created by the word of His mouth, and He said it was "good." This means that God's thinking was good and so was His heart. Man was created in the image of God. The condition of our hearts will show up in what we say also. The mouth is the gauge for the health of our minds. "Let no corrupt communication proceed out of your mouth, but that which is good to the use of edifying, that it may minister grace unto the hearers" (Eph. 4:29). The Bible tells us that "the tongue is a little member [of our bodies], and boasteth great things" (James 3:5).

If we communicate praise to God, then we can have the Lord and salvation, blessings and life. We must use great care and caution in what we say and not allow "corrupt communication" to proceed from our mouths. Satan enters our hearts through what we say and then takes over. Since our hearts are vessels, we may choose what those vessels will contain. We must choose carefully.

Now let us discuss the things which bring sickness to our hearts.

Hatred

Hatred will lead us to failure. It will cause a negative attitude, and we will become jealous and envious of others and obstruct the way for God's answers to our prayers. Hatred will drive us into the prison of "self," totally obstructing growth in our life of faith. Jesus emphasized that we must get rid of hatred: "And when ye stand praying, forgive, if ye have ought against any: that your Father also which is in heaven may forgive you your trespasses. But if ye do not forgive, neither will your Father which is in heaven forgive your trespasses" (Mark 11:25-26).

Hatred is a negative attitude and becomes an obstruction to God's grace.

Many Christians come to me and say, "Pastor, I attend the fasting and prayer meetings and the all-night prayer meetings, but my prayers are not answered. How can I receive an answer to my prayers?"

When I look into the details of their problem, I always find them at odds with those who are closest to them—discord between couples, disagreement between parents and children, or trouble between neighbors. Their hearts are full of hatred.

Before human action, there is the thought process in the mind of the person who takes the action. If I hate others, the feeling of hatred rises up in my mind. Consequently, before I hate or curse others, the thought of cursing forms in my mind. So my heart first becomes tainted with cursing and hatred. Then, although I receive assurance in prayer with the faith of God and confess it with my mouth, I cannot receive an answer for my prayer.

God is light and there is no darkness in Him at all. God has a positive heart overflowing with faith, hope and love. If our hearts are tainted with negative thoughts like hatred, curses and grudges, God cannot dwell in the temple of our hearts, and if God departs from us, we cannot receive anything from Him, no matter how hard we may plead.

Where there is hatred, destruction and death will follow. On His last visit to Jerusalem to be crucified, Jesus visited Bethany where Mary and Martha lived with their brother, Lazarus. On that occasion Mary broke an alabaster jar of ointment of spikenard and anointed the feet of Jesus, wiping His feet with her hair. The house was filled with the fragrance of the ointment. Jesus was facing a cruel death on the cross within a few days, and Mary's act was very comforting to Him. All the people who were there and saw the scene felt their hearts overflowing with love and indescribable holiness. No one reproached Mary for what she did, except Judas Iscariot, and he hated her. He rebuked her with a voice full of contempt and anger: "Why was not this ointment sold for three hundred pence, and given to the poor?" (John 12:5). Some of the disciples joined Judas Iscariot in his reproach of Mary.

Then Jesus commended Mary: "Why trouble ye the woman? for she hath wrought a good work upon me. For ye have the poor always with you; but me ye have not always. For in that she hath poured this ointment on my body, she did it for my burial. Verily, I say unto her, Wheresoever this gospel shall be preached in the whole world, there shall also this, that this woman hath done, be told for a memorial of her" (Matt. 26:10-13).

Jesus was comforted even more in commending Mary. But this made Judas Iscariot hate Mary even more, and he extended his hatred to Jesus. He eventually sold Jesus and then committed suicide because of the agony of his guilty conscience. When hatred enters a person's heart, it causes such a negative attitude that the person's thinking, language, seeing and hearing become so biased that blessing departs and he is flooded with trials that can destroy him.

Hitler's atrocities committed in World War II came from hatred. When he was a small boy, his father traveled frequently because of his business. His mother had an illicit love affair with a Jew who lived in the neighborhood during the extended periods when her husband was gone. Hatred toward the man who was his mother's illicit lover boiled up in young Hitler's heart. When he came to power, the accumulating blind hate erupted in his heart, driving him to sacrifice the lives of six million Jews on the altar of his hatred. Then he killed himself.

Hate does the work of stealing, killing and destroying anything it touches. It takes on the characteristics of Satan and is pleased over the misery of its victims. The most devastating part of hatred, however, is its self-destructiveness; for when a man harbors hatred in his heart, he becomes negative. Thus he himself becomes the first victim of his own hatred. In the Bible we read: "A sound heart is the life of the flesh: but envy the rottenness of the bones" (Prov. 14:30).

If we do not get rid of hatred, we can expect no answer to our prayers; nor can we expect any success in life. "Therefore if thine enemy hunger, feed him" (Rom. 12:20). "Love your enemies" (Matt. 5:44).

It is not for the sake of our enemies that Jesus told us we must love our enemies. It is because, if we hate our enemies, we become the victims. Jesus wanted us to be blessed and prosperous. Jesus did not curse His enemies even when He was bleeding and dying on the cross, but He prayed, "Father, forgive them; for they know not what they do" (Luke 23:34).

Hatred is the first element which brings failure in our lives. We must exert our best efforts to keep our heart from being possessed by this disastrous emotion.

Anger

The second attitude which brings failure is anger. This destructive emotion stops our thinking processes and goes so far as to cause heart attacks by constricting the blood vessels of the entire body. It has the power to destroy us within a very short time.

Dr. John Hunter, the famous English surgeon and anatomist, maintained that anger has the power to destroy the person who harbors it. While he was presenting a paper on this subject at an academic seminar, he became involved in an argument and his anger became so strong that he had a heart attack and died on the spot. The Bible says that anger debases a man's character, turning him into an ignorant person: "The discretion of a man deferreth his anger, and it is his glory to pass over a transgression" (Prov. 19:11). "He that is slow to wrath is of great understanding: but he that is hasty of spirit exalteth folly" (Prov. 14:29). "Cease from anger, and forsake wrath: fret not thyself in any wise to do evil" (Ps. 37:8).

Our wrath usually ends with evil. God stands on the side of him who avoids evil. When the people of Israel went toward the land of Canaan, led by Moses, they were in great difficulty because they could not find water in the desert. They complained to Moses with bitterness, and Moses became angry with them. As a result of Moses' anger, he smote the rock twice with his rod, saying, "Hear now, ye rebels; must we fetch you water out of this rock?" (Num. 20:10). Water gushed out of the rock and satisfied the thirst of the children of Israel, but God was displeased with Moses. "Because ye believed me not, to sanctify me in the eyes of the children of Israel, therefore ye shall not bring this congregation into the land which I have given them" (Num. 20:12).

Moses' anger effectively hid God's holiness, and his punishment was that God did not allow him to enter the promised land. Many people today are excluded from a promised land of blessing too, because they allow their anger to mask the holiness of God. "For the wrath of man worketh not the righteousness of God" (James 1:20).

Anger is a negative emotion and blocks the flow of blessing from God. Anger causes broken homes, broken friendships, broken relations between neighbors and even broken health. Anger is a very destructive passion. We must free ourselves of this destructive force.

First, when we become angry, we should try to sing hymns. When we sing hymns, the Holy Spirit will work peace in our hearts and subdue the anger which we are unable to subdue ourselves.

Second, when one becomes angry, he should calmly say, "Let's postpone this anger for just twenty minutes." The devil is impatient, but the Holy Spirit is not. While waiting for twenty minutes the anger will be completely gone, and peace will come instead with the realization that we have done what is right.

Third, when anger is hot, try to understand the reason or object of that passion. Anger is often the result of self-centered thinking. If we are able to understand the reason for our anger, it may disappear and things will go smoothly.

If we can avoid anger, then the Holy Spirit will abide in our hearts in peace and bring forth an abundance of fruit in our lives.

Covetousness

A spirit of covetousness causes us to love other things more than we love God. If covetousness enters our hearts, the blessings of heaven are withheld from us and the wrath of God comes upon us instead, for covetousness is the same as idolatry: "Mortify therefore your members which are upon the earth; fornication, uncleanness, inordinate affection, evil concupiscence, and covetousness, which is idolatry: for which things' sake the wrath of God cometh on the children of disobedience" (Col. 3:5-6).

We must not misinterpret covetousness as a vision from God to attain our desires and goals. Covetousness is different from vision. Covetousness is a selfish desire for someone else's position, possessions or place in life. Even if we love our husbands, wives, children, possessions or job more than God, covetousness is already in our hearts. Covetousness seeks to glorify self through greed. But a vision which God instills in the heart causes one to glorify God with all the power available to him, as he works and prays to bring his vision into reality. The devil sows covetousness in our hearts to steal God's blessing from us and eventually kill us. One reason why some businessmen cannot succeed in their undertakings is because of covetousness. If an enterprise does well, the entrepreneur often becomes covetous and expands his business beyond his capability, thus bringing ruin upon himself. Accordingly, anything which begins with a covetous motive inevitably fails, for the Holy Spirit cannot take part in it.

Covetousness enters our lives in several phases. The first phase is pride. Pride comes as a consequence of inordinate self-love, which causes us to forget our rightful duty to God. It originated with Satan. The proud man, elevating himself before God, satisfies his inordinate desire to make himself his idol. God will not tolerate the proud person nor walk with him.

The second phase is lying. To satisfy their covetousness, people slander in order to magnify themselves. He who easily tells a lie is a man whose heart is full of greed. The Bible says over and over again that God loves righteousness and honesty. A person who tells lies cannot walk with God.

Covetousness brought the death sentence to our father Adam, made countless mortals undergo the judgment of God and stained history with blood. Covetousness works today to cause splits in churches, contention and destruction. If we want God within us, we must completely rid ourselves of the spirit of covetousness.

Perfectionism

If we stick to perfectionism throughout our lives and insist that all those around us should conform to the standards we set, we will be unable to avoid failure in our families and social lives. If we are preoccupied with insisting, "I am the best, so you should do as I do," division will come to everything we do. When we are reconciled to friends and relatives, and accept their ways with tolerance and generosity, we will find genuine delight in life.

Jesus taught us the important role of an understanding spirit in our lives, through the example of a woman taken in the act of adultery (John 8:3-11). The Pharisees and the teachers of the law appearing in this account were perfectionists who tried to judge everything by the measure of the law. They didn't have the ability to understand the miserable woman, but only had eyes to see her criminal act which had broken their law. Since such people judge everything by the measure of the law, they will always judge others and point out their faults.

Jesus had compassion and mercy toward the woman. He saw her not in the light of the law, but in the light of mercy. He saw the path which she had walked until she reached the point of committing such a sin. He also envisioned her in the future as a born-again person. In John 3:17 we read, "For God sent not his Son into the world to condemn the world, but that the world through him might be saved."

Our outlook on the world about us will differ greatly according to whether we view it with a positive or negative outlook. If we see everything and everyone through eyes of mercy, considering ourselves as though we had been in the situation and Jesus had forgiven us, we will forgive the faults of others and accept them as they are. Furthermore, we will even bear their faults and burdens. If we live with compassion for others, understanding and accepting them, constructive and productive results will follow us in our lives. We are all sinners who have been forgiven by God and are serving God now to the best of our ability.

In Yellowstone National Park in the United States, the wild animals are allowed to live in the open fields. Every morning animals like wolves, foxes and weasels come to a big dumping ground to eat. When a bear arrives on the scene, they all move away and watch the bear eat. The bears are so large and ferocious that all the other animals are afraid of them—except the tiny skunk. A skunk will eat right beside the bear and the bear will pay no attention to it. A skunk cannot begin to rival the bear in strength, but the bear knows that if he makes one hostile move the skunk will eject a very offensive odor that will remain on the bear's body for a long time. This causes the bear to behave as if he did not see the skunk. Even the clumsy bear has the wisdom to avoid something unpleasant.

Many people today live in self-righteousness, and they quarrel about things which usually are not important. Such conflicts should be avoided for the sake of peace. They are in some ways like the skunk. After becoming part of a problem they experience rupture in their personalities, resulting in loneliness. Perfectionism is not one of the attributes of God. If God were to judge this world through the eyes of a perfectionist, no one could stand before Him, for there is no one on the face of this earth who is perfect.

We must give up perfectionism so that we may bear the fruit of prosperity, with God in our hearts.

Guilty Conscience

The fifth characteristic which leads to failure is a guilty conscience. It is natural to feel guilty if we commit an act which is against ethics or social law or is a sin against God. We ought to be penitent. We are made alive as Christians when we accept Jesus Christ as Savior and we can always know whether God is pleased or grieved with us, because we continually keep spiritual fellowship with God. We also know that if we commit a sin God's presence lifts from our hearts, and the only way to be restored to His fellowship is to become penitent.

When we confess our sins and sincerely repent, God forgives our sins and removes the guilt, restoring joy and peace in our hearts. If we are still oppressed by a continuing guilty conscience, then we have become a victim of our enemy, Satan.

If we want to be rid of a guilty conscience, we must cleanse our hearts of past sins, forgive ourselves also and then forget them. Christians who cannot feel free from guilt because of sins committed before their spiritual rebirth need to be freed from all traces of the guilt with which Satan would love to keep them weighted down. The Word tells us, "If we confess our sins, he is faithful and just to forgive us our sins, and to cleanse us from all unrighteousness" (1 John 1:9). "And their sins and iniquities will I remember no more. Now where remission of these is, there is no more offering for sin'' (Heb. 10:17-18).

Man is unable to forgive and forget sin easily. Only the precious blood of Jesus can wash our sins away and erase them from our memory. A guilty conscience keeps us far away from God.

When I was starting my pioneer church right after graduation from seminary, I had been filled with the Holy Spirit and was really feeling good and content that I was abiding in Jesus. But when I became involved in some dispute, I felt that I had stepped out of the Lord's will. I would fall on my knees in repentance. Through confession I would once again be restored to freedom in my spirit. Then I was in sweet fellowship with my Lord once more. However, the following morning, I would feel that somehow I had failed to find my rightful relationship with God. My spirit felt so heavy from this up-and-down living that I could no longer bear it, so I cried out to the Lord for a solution to my problem.

"Lord, I want to be in fellowship with You all the time. Let me not be in fellowship one hour and out of fellowship the next hour!"

Then the Holy Spirit said to me, "How long did you pray before you received your family name 'Cho'?"

"I have never prayed such a prayer, Lord."

"Then how did you receive that name?"

"I was born into the Cho clan."

"Have you been born again by believing in Jesus as your Savior?"

"Yes."

"You said that you were born into the Cho clan, didn't you?"

"Yes."

"Then is it possible that your family name is Cho when you are happy, and that it changes to Kim when you are not happy?"

(No answer.)

"As your family name is Cho no matter how you feel, if you were born again as a child of God through believing in Jesus as your Savior, you are still a child of God and a member of the family of God no matter whether you 'feel' that you are or not."

(Again, no answer.)

Hearing this word, my conflict was resolved and I could understand this scripture: "But of him are ye in Christ Jesus, who of God is made unto us wisdom, and righteousness, and sanctification, and redemption" (1 Cor. 1:30).

If we have Jesus abiding within as our Savior, we are always in fellowship with Him. When Jesus was crucified, we were crucified with

Him. When He was buried in the tomb, we were also buried with Him; and when He was resurrected, we were resurrected. We left all our sins nailed to the cross. The Bible clearly says, "There is therefore now no condemnation to them which are in Christ Jesus" (Rom. 8:1).

Jesus took our guilt upon Himself on the cross. Now there can be no condemnation to those who are in Jesus. Since we are human beings, we commit sins sometimes, but we are cleansed through repentance. So there is no condemnation for us.

A guilty conscience is a heavy burden which can destroy our lives. It makes us sad and depressed and deprives us of courage and hope. It keeps our hearts from receiving God's grace. We should get rid of this guilty conscience and be free in Jesus.

Fear

The sixth condition which brings failure to our lives is a negative emotion which we can call care, anxiety or fear.

Normal healthy fear is right and good. The fear of fire makes us cautious when using fire and the fear of an automobile makes us observe the necessary traffic regulations. The fear of punishment helps us keep the law of the land. It is not desirable, however, that we should be anxious and fearful over things which cannot harm us.

If we are uneasy in our hearts, we are not happy and our life will not be in balance. When a restless person enters his own home, complaints and bitterness follow him. Wherever that unhappy person goes, a chain reaction of unrest pursues.

A large number of people among us live in constant fear and distress. When these feelings intensify enough, fear possesses their hearts, making everything they see and hear to be totally negative. Fear brings a state of atrophy to their minds and bodies and causes sickness.

Dr. Walt Clement Alberts, a physician at the Mayo Clinic, made public a special report that all kinds of gastroenteric disorders start with unrest in the inner attitudes.

A famous American who advocated the philosophy of success was Napoleon Hill. He pointed out that seven types of fear destroy man. The most prevalent is fear of poverty, the second is fear of criticism, and the third is the fear of sickness. Fourth on Hill's list is fear of the loss of love. Since man has a soul, love is as essential as food. Fifth on the list is fear of old age. This is fear of being pushed into the background. Number six is fear of losing freedom. People who have gone through war, like the Koreans, have much greater fear of losing freedom. Last on the list of fears is the fear of death.

Where do such fears come from? When Adam ate the forbidden fruit, he knew that he was naked and hid himself among the trees of the garden because he felt shame. When God looked for Adam and asked him why he was hiding, Adam answered, "I heard thy voice in the garden and I was afraid, because I was naked; and I hid myself" (Gen. 3:10).

Adam ate the forbidden fruit probably expecting that his eyes would be opened and he would suddenly become a god. He had a desire to live independently, free from God's protection. But when he was actually free from God as a result of eating the forbidden fruit, the first thing that hit him was shame. Instead of a brilliant future, he saw his body. This was original shame which could never be hidden in any way unless God covered it with His grace. What Adam saw was a clod of dirt which had been crushed.

Next, Adam was a victim of the fear that he couldn't live alone in the still woods for an hour. Adam feared the future and his surroundings. He was frightened; he had lost his confidence. There was an immediate and frightening change in his environment. The animals which had been meek and docile suddenly became ferocious, and the beautiful garden suddenly changed into a hostile place.

Adam's fear was an indication that the love and care of God had departed. As long as he lived in fear, the love, faith and hope of God could not dwell in his heart.

Then there is that which comes inevitably—the wrath of God. The Bible reads thus: "There is no fear in love; but perfect love casteth out fear: because fear hath torment. He that feareth is not made perfect in love" (1 John 4:18).

Fear is the result of the oppression by the devil. Idolaters are afraid of the retaliation of the devil. The devil always steals, kills, destroys and has nothing to do with blessing. The supreme goal of those who are oppressed by Satan here on earth is to avoid harm. Fear hath torment!

God never works with anyone who has fear in his heart. When the people of Israel went out of Egypt and came to Kadesh-Barnea, near the land of Canaan, Moses chose twelve men and sent them to search out the land. When they returned, ten of them gave a report that was full of fear: "Nevertheless the people be strong that dwell in the land, and the cities are walled, and very great: and moreover we saw the children of Anak there....We be not able to go up against the people; for they are stronger than we...and there we saw the giants...and we were in our own sight as grasshoppers, and so we were in their sight'' (Num. 13:28-33).

We can once again find the fallen image of Adam in their report. Despite the fact that all their food, clothes and shelter had been miraculously provided up to that time through the goodness of God, at the most critical moment they took the position, ''We be not able to go up against the people.'' When man asserts himself, demanding his independence from God, he cannot help being afraid. Joshua and Caleb, however, were trusting in God, so they said boldly: ''The land, which we passed through to search it, is an exceeding good land. If the Lord delight in us, then he will bring us into this land, and give it to us; a land flowing with milk and honey'' (Num. 14:7-8).

And the scouts ascertained that it was a good land. They had indeed returned with proof that it was a good land. They brought a branch with a cluster of grapes so large that it had to be carried between two men on a pole. The ten scouts, on the other hand, were afraid. They had put their trust in themselves while the other two had put their trust in God. The ten scouts made all the people so fearful that the children of Israel wept all night and selected another leader to lead them back to slavery in Egypt. They made God very angry with them. God was so angry that He told them that Joshua and Caleb, the two who had given the good report, were the only two people who would live to see the promised land. Because of their fear the people had to live out their lives in the wilderness without seeing the promised land.

Now we should clearly understand the source and results of fear so that we have the answer to overcome it. Fear comes from taking our eyes off God and depending on our limited abilities. Our attitude should be to keep our eyes on God and learn to depend on Him. We should not look at our surroundings and allow them to dictate our feelings of fear or trust, thus placing our hope in outward appearances. This was the difference between two who trusted God and the ten who did not.

King Saul and the people of Israel were greatly afraid when nine-foot Goliath challenged them, wielding a spear like the staff of a weaver's beam. But David had grown up trusting in God. Recalling his experience of killing a lion while a shepherd, he was not afraid. As he now stood before Goliath with five smooth stones, David did not look at the fact that he was only a seventeen-year-old youth. He kept his eyes on God, the creator of the universe, whom he had learned to know well.

In order that we may be delivered from fear, we should know through experience that God, who made the heavens and the earth and all things in them, loves and protects us like the apple of His eye. Then we will develop the strong conviction that God is in us and that He has become our own Father, and soon fear will be driven from our hearts as we trust in Him.

No human being in this world has ever overcome fear without living in close fellowship with God, for fear originates at the point when man departs from God, and it will never disappear until he returns to God. "There is no peace, saith the Lord, unto the wicked" (Is. 48:22).

Those who neither know God nor believe in Jesus live their transient life in the midst of ceaseless uncertainty and fear because their sins have not been forgiven. Since our God is a God of forgiveness, and we came seeking His forgiveness, all our sins are forgiven and we have received rest and peace from Him.

Frustration

Frustration brings failure to our lives. When people have difficulty in their relationships with others, or when they fail in business ventures and other undertakings, they brand themselves as failures and fall into feelings of inferiority, allowing themselves to give in to despair. When we are not apparently succeeding, failure begins to creep over all other areas of our lives.

During our lives we meet with different circumstances. On each occasion we endeavor to find the most suitable answer for each situation. This solution-finding method can be compared to a series of doors. In our struggle to find the right door, we sometimes bump against the walls and posts of indifference and difficulty or we stumble over other obstacles. Hasty people bump against difficulties more frequently and harder, and calm people bump less. No one is completely exempt from this painful experience.

What decides success or failure of our lives is our attitude when we face failure—whether we get up and try again or quit trying. There are a lot of successful people around us who were at one time unsuccessful at something, but they did not give up. They tried again and kept on trying until they finally succeeded.

J.M. Whistler, the famous American painter, experienced the despair of a door closing in his face. He entered West Point with a shining ambition and studied hard. Unfortunately, he failed in chemistry. When he graduated from the military institution, his beautiful dream was smashed.

After struggling for a while in the depths of depression and inferiority, Whistler decided to become an engineer. He enrolled in a school of technology and studied diligently, but his fingers fumbled so badly that he became an object of ridicule and was expelled. His worst problem was that he was unable to make ends meet because not one door opened to him. In the midst of his desperate situation, he realized that only Jesus could become his door. So he fell on his knees and prayed: "Lord, the doors are all closed to me. There is nothing opening. Lord Jesus, You are the only way open to me. Lead me."

Whistler then started painting as a pastime, but finding that he had a gift for painting he continued with it as a serious occupation. His paintings sold like hotcakes, and before long he became a famous portrait painter who enjoyed a good reputation all over Europe and the United States.

Another example is Phillips Brooks, a pastor who wrote the well-known Christmas carol "O Little Town of Bethlehem." After graduation from a normal school, he became a teacher. He was devoted to his teaching and taught with much sincerity, but his pupils were disobedient and unceasingly caused problems. He was forced to move from one school to another until finally there was no other place for him to go except to church.

There Brooks was encouraged to go to seminary and study to become a pastor, but he did not want to become a pastor. For a livelihood, however, he was forced to do just that. He entered a seminary and became a pastor. As soon as he stood behind the pulpit, the power of God suddenly came upon him and his voice sounded like that of an angel. When he preached, a large number of people were moved to tears and gave their hearts to the Lord.

The apostle Paul also thoroughly experienced the despair of a closed door. He once set his face to preach the gospel in Bithynia. Paul thought that if he preached the gospel there, it would then flood into Africa and Asia. He should get there as soon as he could and preach the gospel, he thought, for that was the place where his dream could be realized. Thinking this, Paul was impatient. He announced his plan to the churches and asked for their prayers and support. Strangely enough, when Paul tried to leave, his departure was delayed first by one thing and then another. It was not the interference of the devil.

"Now when they had gone throughout Phrygia and the region of Galatia, and were forbidden of the Holy Ghost to preach the word in Asia, after they were come to Mysia, they assayed to go into Bithynia:

but the Spirit suffered them not" (Acts 16:6-7).

Paul went down to Troas where he really did not want to go. He went depressed and in despair, but he continued to pray, ridding himself of his frustration through prayer. Then a new door was opened to him. It was a bigger and brighter door than Bithynia: "And a vision appeared to Paul in the night; there stood a man of Macedonia, and prayed him, saying, Come over into Macedonia, and help us. And after he had seen the vision, immediately we endeavored to go into Macedonia, assuredly gathering that the Lord had called us for to preach the gospel unto them" (Acts 16:9-10).

Paul was directed to go to Macedonia, which was the last place he ever considered. He now realized that it was God's design.

There is no living person whose dreams have not been shattered at some time in life. A great many people, while trying to fulfill their dreams, find frustration or closed doors and go down to their "Troas" instead and stay there! Then they waste their whole lives blaming their circumstances, neighbors and friends. But we will find a new door and live a better life if we, like Paul, pray in our "Troas" and come to God with a positive attitude, saying, "Father, I stretch my hands to Thee; no other help I know." The Bible says, "Is any among you afflicted? Let him pray" (James 5:13).

When we experience failure or frustration, we should pray as Elijah did. Even after destroying 450 prophets of Baal, when Jezebel threatened to kill him, Elijah fled for his life. He went a day's journey into the wilderness where he sat down under a juniper tree and cried out to God for help. Then God heard Elijah's prayer and gave him new strength.

Jesus is both our shepherd and our door through which we can go in and out and find wonderful pasture: "I am the door: by me if any man enter in, he shall be saved, and shall go in and out, and find pasture" (John 10:9).

When we fall on our knees and pray to Jesus after tasting the bitter cup of failure, Jesus becomes a far better door for us. Beyond the door there is prepared a wonderful world, surpassing our fondest dreams: "But as it is written, Eye hath not seen, nor ear heard, neither have entered into the heart of man, the things which God hath prepared for them that love him" (1 Cor. 2:9).

This means that good things we have never seen nor heard nor thought of are prepared for those who do not stop at "Troas." Such people build their altar of prayer and fall on their knees for God's direction. Therefore, if your dream of going to a "Bithynia" is broken, just take the broken pieces in your hand and go to your "Troas." The city of "Troas" may become your splendid starting point.

We have considered seven elements which bring failure to our lives and we have received answers for them. If we are sober and watchful in our everyday living, we will be raised to the next step leading to prosperity. It is regrettable to see a person who does not make the most of a large fortune he has inherited from his parents but wastes it away. We should always be examining our hearts in faith lest we annul "the blessing of prosperity" which is the inheritance Jesus bought for us with His blood.

For a Successful Life

Without exception, everyone living in this world wants to live a successful life because true happiness and meaning of life can only be found in the success which God gives. A life of prosperity is the same as a successful life.

God wants His children to live a successful life and enjoy happiness and pleasure. As manifested in His process of creation, God wants success for everyone. Everyone who has been created in the image and likeness of God has been blessed with the ability and privilege of living a successful life. This is the ultimate will and purpose of God for us. "Open thy mouth wide, and I will fill it" (Ps. 81:10). "And God is able to make all grace abound toward you; that ye, always having all sufficiency in all things, may abound to every good work" (2 Cor. 9:8). "Every man also to whom God hath given riches and wealth, and hath given him power to eat thereof, and to take his portion, and to rejoice in his labor; this is the gift of God" (Eccl. 5:19). "Beloved, I wish above all things that thou mayest prosper and be in health, even as thy soul prospereth" (3 John 2).

From Genesis to Revelation, the Word of God is filled with examples of great men who lived successful lives, including Abraham, Isaac, Jacob, Moses and the judges. Even the lives of Job and Jonah, which seemed to be failures for a moment, end with success. In the New Testament we see the changed life of an illiterate Peter, and the truly successful life of Paul, who counted all things but loss for the excellency of the knowledge of Christ Jesus. He considered whatever things he might have boasted about as mere refuse. The place God has prepared for Christians is described in the book of Revelation. This book also illustrates how earnestly God wants our lives to prosper. Therefore we should understand clearly that it is pleasing to God that we live a successful life.

What does a "successful life" mean? Modern man has a tendency to measure success merely in the accumulation of material wealth, but there are other kinds of success which God gives. Whatever work we may be engaged in, if we receive satisfaction, pleasure, self-development and achievement and it brings glory to God—that is a successful life because of His accomplishment of that success in us. When a businessman gains profit in his business, when a scholar bears fruit from his study, when a preacher succeeds in proclaiming the gospel, when a politician or statesman succeeds in bringing economic prosperity to his nation—though they work in different fields, each of them has led a successful life.

Let us consider several secrets each of us can use and apply in our own fields for a successful life.

Discern the Will of God

Life is just like a ship sailing on the ocean. Our goal in life should be like a ship sailing full speed, heading in a definite direction. As a baseball pitcher cannot lead the team to victory unless he can effectively direct the ball at the batter, so a man cannot live a successful life unless he has a goal toward which he can effectively direct his efforts.

How can we find the goal for our lives? Which choice will lead us to success when we must choose a goal? How can we find an opening to the goal when the wall of life obstructs us? What is the will of God for us? To live a successful life, we should understand clearly what the will of God is as soon as possible, for the object of our life is to do the known will of God. We will explain the five steps by which we can discern the will of God.

Absolute Obedience

"For as many as are led by the Spirit of God, they are the sons of God" (Rom. 8:14)

We can interpret the above scripture in reverse. It means that every son of God is led by God. The Bible reads, "But ye have received the spirit of adoption, whereby we cry, Abba, Father" (Rom. 8:15).

Therefore we have the privilege of being led by the Spirit of God in our daily lives. In old times Enoch walked with God all his life (Gen. 5:25). Even today God wants to walk with us and show us His will.

We should first be sure that our hearts are honest before God so that we may discern the will of God. We must have an absolutely obedient heart. We may have an attitude that says we will obey the will of God so long as it is convenient. But if it is not convenient, we will not obey. Then God certainly will not show His will to us.

In the church of today, there are many people who have faith like that of Jonah. Jonah accepted the will of God that He would destroy Nineveh, but he did not accept his role of being sent to cry out that the city should repent and avoid destruction. He placed his own will before the will of God. We accept God's way if it is sweet, but we reject it if it seems bitter. Such an attitude becomes the first stumbling block in our walk with God.

Jesus was an example of absolute obedience in His prayer just before His crucifixion: "And he said, Abba, Father, all things are possible unto thee; take away this cup from me: nevertheless not what I will, but what thou wilt" (Mark 14:36).

Samuel sharply rebuked Saul's disobedience: "Hath the Lord as great delight in burnt offering and sacrifices, as in obeying the voice of the Lord? Behold, to obey is better than sacrifice, and to hearken than the fat of rams, for rebellion is as the sin of witchcraft, and stubbornness is as iniquity and idolatry" (1 Sam. 15:22-23).

Therefore obedience is the absolute condition through which the divine will is revealed in our lives. If we come to God with hearts ready for whatever happens, saying, "I will obey the will of God whether it is advantageous to me or not, whether I prosper or perish, and whether I am in good health or not," God certainly will show us His will. If we cry out to God requesting something after making up our mind that we must have it, our prayer will not be answered, for our will has been put before the will of God. When we calmly and earnestly pray to know the will of God, and we are free from lust, God will show His will for our lives.

Our Greatest Desire

If we pray to know the will of God, He will cause us to have desires according to His will. God is not far away from us in a remote heaven. Nor is He a person who only appeared in the temple at Jerusalem 2,000 years ago. God is within us now, walking with us each day. The Bible says, "For it is God which worketh in you both to will and to do of his good pleasure" (Phil. 2:13).

Therefore, in order to know the will of God, we should watch carefully to see which desire is rising up while we pray. When God shows His will to us, He does not do it against our will, but He arouses a desire in our hearts, making our wills agree with His will.

I receive many requests to speak in revival meetings all over the world. If I were to accept all those requests, it would be impossible for me to minister at my church. So I spread the invitations before me and pray,

"Lord, I can't accept more than four of these. Which ones should I accept? This one is from the United Kingdom, that one is from France and this is from the United States of America." Then I pray earnestly all night, with fasting, and God places in my heart a desire agreeing with His will, through the Holy Spirit. The invitations that I accept are chosen by the voice which comes out of my heart while I am praying. Sometimes the country I very much wanted to go to is not chosen, and another country which I felt reluctant to consider is chosen. Nevertheless, since I have made up my mind to obey God's will absolutely, I am able to choose in accordance with the desires of the Holy Spirit.

In 1969, when our church was considering the move to Yoido to build a new sanctuary accommodating 10,000 people, I was in doubt as to whether this was the Lord's will. At that time the cost of construction was estimated at two billion won, but our church could only finance two million won. Therefore, if it had not been in the Lord's will for us to move ahead with the building, my church might have gone bankrupt and would have pulled me down with it, hiding God's glory.

At that critical hour, I knelt down before God and made an earnest supplication. I emptied my heart of all thoughts, plans and lust. Then I knelt in complete subjection. Suddenly, in the midst of my prayer the presence of the Holy Spirit, like liquid fire, rose up in my heart and a strong desire came to me. There was nothing in my hands, nor was there anything heard or visible. Yet I could feel in my heart a strong desire springing up to build a church that would accommodate 10,000 people, that would send missionaries beyond the five oceans and to the six continents. We started with empty hands and within five years we built the church that could accommodate 10,000 people. We have paid all the debts of that building program and we are preaching the gospel to the whole world through our missionaries.

Our *desire* is such a vital part in discerning the will of God. We must pray for the solutions to our problems with fasting, being willing to stay up all night if necessary, observing closely the strong and clear desire arising in our hearts.

With the Word of God

When a desire arises in our hearts, we need to examine it in the light of God's Word to learn whether this desire is consistent with the will of God. No revelation should ever be allowed to override the Bible. The Word of God becomes the supreme measure and final authority by which all matters can be judged. When Jesus was tempted by Satan in the wilderness He put Satan to flight by quoting Scripture beginning with, "It is written...."

However strong a desire may be in our hearts, unless it conforms to the Word of God, it is not coming from the Holy Spirit. In our hearts desires come not only from the Holy Spirit. Fleshly lusts, greed and wicked desires also arise from our soulish nature and from Satan.

A man who was newly appointed as the director of a choir in the United States had a beautiful, exemplary family. In the choir was an unusually pretty girl to whom the director was strongly attracted. He was so fascinated by this girl that he reached a point where he could no longer control his emotions. That day he knelt down before God and prayed: "Lord, reveal Your will to me. Let me take it to be Your will that my wife and I were an ill-matched couple from the start, and that it was preordained in heaven for me to have as my wife that charming girl with whom I am falling in love."

That was a very bad prayer! One day the choir director heard the voice of the devil, disguised as the voice of God, telling him that his prayer was heard and accepted. The choir director called on the pastor of the church that day and asked to be permitted to divorce his wife. The pastor showed him the scripture, "Let not the husband put away his wife" (1 Cor. 7:11), and tried to convince him of God's wrath. He went ahead with his fleshly desire, however, and divorced his wife and married the pretty girl. Completely disillusioned by her husband's actions, the wife of the choir director gave up her faith in God and remarried.

In a short time, the choir director could no longer pray, since the Holy Spirit had departed from him. He suffered a nervous breakdown. It was then that he realized he had done wrong. He went to the church and wept bitterly, beating the altar with his hands, but his tears could never repair the damage he had done in yielding to the desires of his flesh and rejecting the scriptural counsel of his pastor. The Word of God is our final authority. Anyone who disregards the supreme counsel of the Word of God soon reaches a point where it is impossible for him to go back and make things right.

When a strong desire arises in our hearts, we must judge it in the light of the Word of God. If it is not consistent with the Word of God, we should resolutely renounce it and command it to depart. Revelations, visions, tongues or prophecy which disagree with the Word of God are never from God. Such things which do not come from God are from the devil, no matter how well they are disguised to represent God's will.

All Scripture is the precise Word of God, free from error and written by the inspiration of God, providing us with the standard by which we can see and know clearly what the will of God may be.

Circumstantial Evidence

God is a God of order. He uses certain methods to reveal His will. If a desire arises during your prayer and the desire agrees with the Word of God, then you must pray that God will give you circumstantial evidence to clarify His agreement with your desire.

In the Old Testament, during the life of Elijah, God did not allow rain to fall on the land of His rebellious people in Israel for three-and-a-half years. The long drought and resulting famine drove the Israelites to extreme distress, and their cattle and flocks died because they had nothing to eat. One day, when the land was in the grip of severe drought, Elijah went up to the top of Mount Carmel and threw himself down on his face and prayed earnestly to God. He sent his servant toward the sea to look for a cloud. The servant went but saw no cloud. So Elijah sent him back to look again and again until he had scanned the skies seven times. After the seventh look, the servant returned saying, "Behold, there ariseth a little cloud out of the sea, like a man's hand."

When Elijah heard this, he said to Ahab, "Prepare thy chariot, and get thee down, that the rain will stop thee not" (1 Kings 18:1).

Beyond the Word and Elijah's desire there was a little cloud. When we pray for our desires, we should begin to see a tiny cloud of faith bringing our answer.

Gideon was one of the greatest judges in Israel. Like Elijah, he asked for proof from his circumstances. At that time Israel had been invaded by the Midianites and Israel was very close to becoming a conquered nation. For this reason, the heart of young Gideon was burning with desire to see his people delivered from the oppression of the Midianites. One day an angel of God appeared to Gideon and said that this desire agreed with God's desires. But Gideon still could not be satisfied with the message from the angel. So he asked for evidence: "If thou wilt save Israel by mine hand, as thou hast said, Behold, I will put a fleece of wool in the floor; and if the dew be on the fleece only, and it be dry upon all the earth beside, then shall I know that thou wilt save Israel by mine hand, as thou hast said" (Judg. 6:36-37).

On the following morning Gideon rose up early, picked up the fleece covered with dew and squeezed out a bowl full of water. Then Gideon said unto God, "Let not thine anger be hot against me, and I will speak but this once: let me prove, I pray thee, but this once with the fleece; let it now be dry only upon the fleece, and upon all the ground let there be dew'' (Judg. 6:39).

That night God answered Gideon again, doing what he asked. The fleece was dry and all the ground around it was wet with dew. After seeing these evidences in his circumstances, Gideon went out and boldly fought against the Midianites and became God's instrument to save Israel. When God shows us His will He always reveals circumstantial evidence also, whether a tiny cloud or a wet fleece. We can and should pray to receive circumstantial evidence from God for our requests.

Peace in Your Mind When You Pray

When we see circumstantial evidence, it is time to pray for God's peace. Where Satan is, there will be uneasiness. Where God is, there will be peace. Whatever trials and temptations may come to us, if the Spirit of God dwells in us, peace becomes our evidence of agreement with God's will. The work of the Holy Spirit of God will not appear where there is no love and peace.

Those who spread complaints and discontent wherever they go are those who have received another spirit instead of the Holy Spirit. Even though they may attend church, they cause trouble, dissension and uneasiness. The work of the Holy Spirit is to bring love and peace. So the final evidence by which we can discern the will of God is having peace in our hearts and minds. We may have had four other evidences that we are moving in God's will until we approach this last evidence. If the final evidence is lacking, it is an indication that this may be God's will but the timing is not right. If we experience this, we should wait until we have peace in our hearts and minds, because the Holy Spirit brings peace when God's perfect time has come. "Then are they glad because they be quiet; so he bringeth them unto their desired haven" (Ps. 107:30).

God rules all of His creation according to His seasons. The Bible reads, "To every thing there is a season, and a time to every purpose under the heaven" (Eccl. 3:1). The season and time mentioned here concerning the will of God can be decided by judging whether you have peace when you pray. Unless you have peace when you pray, it is not the right time for you to pursue the thing you are praying for. But if peace flows like a river, you may understand that it is a sign to take action. Because you have peace, you may be assured that God's will is being accomplished.

We have seen the five stages in which we can discern the will of God. First, have the attitude of mind that you will do whatever God wants you to do in total obedience. Second, through your prayer, try to see which desire God causes to arise in your heart. Third, refer it to the Word of God to find whether it is consistent with the Word. Fourth, ask earnestly for circumstantial evidence. Fifth, wait until you have peace of mind and heart, and then proceed. These five stages will become the steps which will help you to move successfully in the will of God.

Life With a Goal

If you have seen the will of God clearly, you should use the revealed will of God as your goal in life. Having a goal in life gives life more structure and intensity. A goal also brings more abundant results from our lives. But life without an objective is like a fallen leaf floating aimlessly on the water until it finally sinks.

While we should have one great aim which we will pursue throughout all periods of our lives, we should also have smaller objectives which we plan to attain. A detailed schedule and plan for each day should be made showing which we are going to carry out first. The apostle Paul referred to these large and small aims as those for "which I am apprehended of Christ Jesus." He used the expression, "pressing toward the mark," to depict life in which all of one's efforts are exerted to attain a goal. "But I follow after, if that I may apprehend that for which also I am apprehended of Jesus Christ. Brethren, I count not myself to have apprehended but this one thing I do; forgetting those things which are behind, and reaching forth unto those things which are before, I press toward the mark for the prize of the high calling of God in Christ Jesus" (Phil. 3:12-14).

A goal-oriented attitude becomes a tonic which vitalizes our faith and our lives. Now let's examine how an aim can be pursued and attained by dividing it into several sections.

A Clear-cut Goal

Most of the people of today's world fail to live successful lives. They wander aimlessly, though they have intelligence, health and education, because they do not have a goal. One day while playing golf, Norman Vincent Peale, the famous American counselor, opened a conversation with the young golf caddie who was carrying Peale's golf clubs:

Peale: How is it going?

Caddie: Well, so-so. Always the same.

Peale: What is the work that you really want to do?

Caddie: Well, I don't know.

Peale: Do you have any specialty?

Caddie: No, I don't have anything that I can do especially well.

Peale: With what kind of job will you be most satisfied?

Caddie: Well, I don't think there is anything which will satisfy me particularly.

Peale: I have just asked you three very important questions, but you gave only vague answers to all of my questions. As soon as you go home today, find a pencil and a piece of paper and don't leave until you can write down the clear answers to my questions. I will see you tomorrow.

On the following day, when Peale met the young man again, he told Peale that he wanted to become a foreman in a factory manufacturing plastics. Eventually, he was promoted to the position of foreman and found a satisfactory life. The most important thing in life is to establish a goal. Though we have so much faith that we could remove mountains, unless we have an objective we are pursuing—"things hoped for" (Heb. 11:1)— our faith is nothing.

Except for some special cases, God recognizes the desires of believers who love Him, and He brings their desires to accomplishment. The following scriptures prove this: "Delight thyself also in the Lord, and he shall give thee the desires of thine heart" (Ps. 37:4). "Therefore I say unto you, What things soever ye desire, when ye pray, believe that ye receive them, and ye shall have them" (Mark 11:24).

We must have an aim in our lives by which God may manifest His glory. We must view our aim in the light of God's Word and implement it with specific details, item by item. God is well pleased with definite plans and prayers.

If a man who has poor eyesight wears incorrect eyeglasses, his vision will be poor and he will be unable to carry out what he wants to do quickly and accurately. Such is the case of a man who does not have a definite aim in life. He will lack the ability to live an effective life. A well-focused, clear aim is the shortcut to prosperity.

A Burning Desire

No matter how high we aim and how elaborately we plan, unless we have a *burning desire* to attain it, our aim is like owning a car that is merely a drawing on a piece of paper. Once we set an aim, we should run with a burning desire and a concentration of mind and heart. A man who has little desire to accomplish cannot achieve any kind of creative work. A man's character is affected more by enthusiasm for his aim in life than by his past achievements or his present life-style. Not only his character, but also the problems of his life and death are determined by the way he pursues his aims.

Dr. George E. Brooks, the world-renowned authority on microbiosis at Tallon Medical College, said: "The quickest way to death is to retire and idle your life away. If you want to continue your life, *you must have an aim* which you can pursue with interest."

Man is a being who pursues an aim. Consequently, the harder a man pursues his aim, the better and more vital his life will be.

A real-life story follows that will support my point: A bereaved woman was left alone with a two-year-old son. She was then stricken with cancer. This mother had a burning desire that she would not die before her son's graduation from college. Through her tremendous will power and her strong desire the woman, whom the doctors had already given up on, lived another 20 years to see her son graduate from college. She died six weeks after his graduation. The force which extended the life of this mother was not good medicine, knowledge or any other material thing. It was her aim based on her love for her son and her burning desire to see him graduate.

In the parable of the judge and the widow, Jesus taught us the power of a burning desire (Luke 18:1-8). This unrighteous judge was insensitive, proud and cruel. He did not fear God, much less man. When the widow kept bothering him with her continual pleas, asking for justice against her adversary, the judge decided to avenge her. Your burning desire to achieve your objective will have such wonderful power, too. The Bible reads thus: "Not slothful in business; fervent in spirit; serving the Lord" (Rom. 12:11).

God does not work miracles for those who do not have a burning desire. The burning desire comes before God in unflagging prayer which works out according to the measure of faith within us, and we attain our goal through miraculous means.

A burning desire to see miracles always increases our faith to believe God for the miracles and see them come to pass. The desire that ought to exist in the hearts of some people is suppressed. There are several reasons for that. The first is fear caused by expectation of failure. He who is afraid of the future cannot take one step forward. Such a person should not expect that his life will be successful. We have an old saying: "If we have done our best, we leave the rest in the hands of God." Without disciplining ourselves to believe God (or have faith) there could be no real burning desire. Even if there seems to be such a desire, it is only a passing daydream.

The second reason is diffidence. The simple and honest fool who has no talent is better off than he who has enough ability and is gifted, but is immersed in feelings of inferiority. Such a person hides his desire for fear that he may fall behind if he participates in anything competitive. This sort of person is prone to excuse himself. A car that is standing still has no power, but when the motor is started there is plenty of power. Ability is not given to a man until he starts a work with a burning desire.

The third way in which such desire is suppressed is by restriction of one's circumstances. One example is an occasion in which parents force their children to live according to their wishes. We can have true success and happiness only when our lives are compatible with our God-given talents and desires to fulfill them.

If we put our plans into practice step-by-step, with a burning desire to achieve our goal, the plans will slowly develop until they are finally a total reality. A burning desire will bring to our hearts a wonderful conviction that we can achieve our goal. Fervent prayer with a burning desire produces a firm conviction that we can believe God in all adverse circumstances, even when there is a lack of external evidence.

Two Laws That Help Us Reach Our Goal

When we run toward our goal with a burning heart, we must keep two laws in mind. One is the "group law" and the other is the "law of sight" (or the law of looking at the goal). These two laws are creative and cosmic.

First, the "group law" is a natural law which is illustrated by the fact that "birds of a feather flock together." Those who have a self-image of being successful, with a clear aim and burning desire, always get together with others who also have a self-image of being successful. But those who are filled with defeat and inferiority seem to join those who are the same kind of people.

Friends and loyal subjects like Jonathan and Joab gathered together with King David, who was courageous and adhered to justice. Intelligent people flocked to wise Solomon. On the other hand, since Rehoboam was very stupid, those who surrounded him were all foolish people. Thus Rehoboam, acting on the advice of such friends, fell into the tragedy of being recorded as a shameful king who left a blot in history. Through his foolishness his kingdom was divided into two parts: the kingdom of Judah and the kingdom of Israel.

If we have a burning desire, those who have a like burning desire will gather together with us. Successful people always talk about positive and hopeful things related to being successful. If we listen to the wisdom of those who have experienced success and put the work in the hands of the right people, our goal can be achieved more easily.

Second, the "law of sight" makes the object of our desire approach us little by little. If we fix our eyes on an object in our minds and look upon it prayerfully and intently through the eyes of faith, then it happens that either the object approaches us or we will move toward it. The fall of Adam and Eve was initiated by looking at the forbidden fruit, and David's sin of adultery with Bathsheba began when he looked at her naked body from the roof of the palace.

Lot's wife became a pillar of salt when she looked back at Sodom and Gomorrah. The lame beggar who lay at the temple gate called Beautiful could stand and leap after he looked at Peter and John. When God blessed Abraham with the promise of a posterity, God told Abraham to look at the stars; and when God gave him the land of Canaan, He told him to look at the land. "And the Lord said unto Abraham, after that Lot was separated from him, Lift up now thine eyes, and look from the place where thou art northward, and southward, and eastward, and westward: for all the land which thou seest, to thee will I give it, and to thy seed forever" (Gen. 13:14-15).

Our wills do not rule our hearts. Our eyes of faith and our imagination do. Imagination is thinking. Seeing is not limited to the vision of the eyes. Through our imagination and our thoughts we can still see when we close our eyes. For this reason the Bible reads: "Keep thy heart with all diligence; for out of it are the issues of life" (Prov. 4:23).

If we look at our goal intently, bringing into captivity every thought to the obedience of Christ, the distance between us and our goal will be shortened, little by little. Finally, we will possess our goal, which in turn possesses us.

The Bible reads: "Finally, brethren, whatsoever things are true, whatsoever things are honest, whatsoever things are just, whatsoever things are pure, whatsoever things are lovely, whatsoever things are of good report; if there be any virtue, and if there be any praise, think on these things" (Phil. 4:8).

Don't Lose Your Peace of Mind: Acknowledge Success

In order to live a successful life, we must not lose our peace of mind. If our hearts wander to and fro like a ship that is tossed by the waves, we cannot succeed in anything. No matter how good our goal may be, how fervent our desire, how well we understand the "group law" and the "law of seeing," if we lose our peace, we cannot aim at our target.

Everything will be in vain.

Our peace of mind is usually broken by covetousness. Of course we should aim high, but we must be willing to begin small too. Even the job of building a great palace begins with one brick. A thousand-mile journey begins with the first step. If tears are stored up, they will eventually make a lake. Vain thoughts cause covetousness, which in turn brings failure by making us forget reality. But if we walk in peace, freeing our hearts of covetousness, the miracle which brings success will happen. Bold faith and conviction—these are important factors which plant peace in our hearts: "And purify your hearts, ye double-minded" (James 4:8). "But let him ask in faith, nothing wavering. For he that wavereth is like a wave of the sea driven with the wind and tossed. For let not that man think that he shall receive anything from the Lord. A double-minded man is unstable in all his ways" (James 1:6-8).

Man was made in the image and likeness of God. God created this world by His Word. Therefore, man who was made in His image and likeness can improve his lot and change his surrounding through his language. Like the Word of God, our language must show the wonderfully creative power of God, spoken in faith.

Jesus came to this world as the Word. This means that God had intended all along to save mankind. Actually, Jesus forgave sins by His word. He healed the sick by His word. He cast out unclean spirits by His word. He made the leaves of the fig tree wither by His word. Peter and John, who had learned the power of speaking out the Word during their three years of following Jesus, made the lame man stand and leap by their words.

Scripture confirms that our language is one of the elements which rules our character and destiny. Through the medium of language we exchange what we think with others. This language is the rope which binds our thinking and our life. A silkworm makes a cocoon with the silk it produces from its mouth. Likewise, a man also controls himself in the way he uses the language which comes out of his mouth. "Thou art snared with the words of thy mouth, thou art taken with the words of thy mouth" (Prov. 6:2). "Even so the tongue is a little member, and boasteth great things" (James 3:5).

Jesus came into this world as the Word and still dwells within us. His Word abides in our hearts and mouths. When we receive Jesus into our hearts, it means the same thing as receiving the Word to our hearts.

The fact that we are born again means that we exchange our language for the language of God. Therefore the Bible says, "For with the heart man believeth unto righteousness; and with the mouth confession is made unto salvation" (Rom. 10:10).

Our speaking should become the language of miracles which gives glory to God, and by it we may share our blessings with our neighbors. Therefore, we should say the following to our neighbors and to God at the same time:

"I am sure I'll be blessed. Jesus made me worthy when He shed His blood for me. So the project I am planning with His approval will certainly succeed."

For others who are struggling, we might say, "Though he is somewhat impetuous, he will become a worthwhile person if he only believes in Jesus. Though he is poor now, he will become more prosperous. I love him, I understand him, and I expect much from him."

And to God, we will want to say, "Oh Lord, thank You, You are the great creator-God. Thank You for Your wonderful works which are changing my life. Thank You that You let the work which I planned work out successfully. Oh Lord, I bless Thee!"

If we acknowledge the power of God with our mouths, it leads our lives to success. If we confess salvation through Jesus with our mouths, salvation will be ours. If we acknowledge blessing, then blessing will come to us.

Today, doctors maintain that since speech affects the entire nervous system, auto-suggestion of confessing with our mouths strongly affects and changes our thinking. This fact was already set forth in James 3:4-5 years ago: "Behold also the ships, which though they be so great, and are driven of fierce winds, yet are they turned about with a very small helm, whithersoever the governor listeth. Even so the tongue is a little member, and boasteth great things."

And the Bible also says, "That whosoever shall say unto this mountain, Be thou removed, and be thou cast into the sea; and shall not doubt in his heart, but shall believe that those things which he saith shall come to pass; he shall have whatsoever he saith" (Mark 11:23).

Jesus said that a miracle would happen to the one who said what he believed, instead of just praying. We can experience the miracle of casting a mountain into the sea, and we can lead a successful life. Therefore, from this moment we first need to have a clear-cut goal and a detailed plan by which we can realize our success in the light of the Word of God.

Second, we need to have a burning desire to see that goal fulfilled.

If we have a fervent desire, we will be highly motivated to do everything we can to bring the goal to fulfillment.

Third, we must paint a brilliant dream of success on the canvas of our minds, using the group law and the law of seeing, knowing that God is glorified when we succeed because He has already approved our goal.

Fourth, we should acknowledge our success with creative language. The confession of our mouth is just like putting a seal on a contract.

The only thing that is left now is to give glory to God after seeing how successfully the plan or goal came to pass. From now on, let God work for you. Mighty wonders will take place!

A Man Is Blessed in All Things

Now we are coming out of the second room, the room of prosperity of circumstances in the house of threefold blessings.

God first made the material world for man before He created him, and then placed man in an abundant and beautiful garden. After the man usurped the sovereignty of God by eating the forbidden fruit, he was forced to live a life of hard work and failure. But our good God intervened and sent His only begotten Son to bear our curse and poverty, to be nailed on the cross in our place. Christ broke that curse and freed us from its bondage.

We who have been blessed in all things should acknowledge the sovereign power of God by giving Him our tithes, the "fruit of the tree of knowledge" in our present age, lest we again come under the curse. We should also use the law of sowing and reaping so that we may receive physical blessings. This is the easy bondage that God laid upon us.

The devil, however, always watches for an opportunity to make the elect of God fall. So we must always free our hearts from hatred, wrath, covetousness, perfectionism, guilty conscience, fear and frustration. Our prosperity depends on having this freedom. Besides, in order that we may live a successful life, we need to discern the will of God as well as live a life with goals that are according to His will.

As God put this good world which He had created into the hands of Adam and Eve, so today Jesus has given us a new world by bearing the curse on the cross for us and removing its bondage. This is the world which leads us to prosperity and blessing. In the beginning Adam and Eve were deprived of their privilege through disobedience and pride. Likewise, if we refuse to acknowledge God's sovereignty, we will invite the bondage of the devil again, who will drag us back into all kinds of failure.

So we are leaving the room called "prosperity" and we are blessed. The evil power of Satan cannot oppress us. We have recovered the power over the world and we have taken dominion again through the grace of Jesus Christ. Our language has the authority of a ruler. Creative wisdom is upon our heads, and we have God in our hearts through the Holy Spirit—all because of Jesus' work of redemption for us.

Those who have already been blessed with prosperity have a new image of themselves. Now that they have been delivered from the curse, they should be able to see the new image of their changed lives as if they were looking into a mirror: "But of him are ye in Christ Jesus, who of God is made unto us wisdom, and righteousness, and sanctification, and redemption" (1 Cor. 1:30).

When we are in Christ Jesus, our sins and curse, together with death, are removed from us and a new portrait of ourselves has been hung: "Blotting out the handwriting of ordinances that was against us, which was contrary to us, and took it out of the way, nailing it to his cross; and having spoiled principalities and powers, he made a shew of them openly, triumphing over them in it" (Col. 2:14-15).

Therefore, we should first look at every problem through the cross, so that we may continuously live a prosperous life. When we look at ourselves, we must see the new self-image which has been created by Christ's work on the cross.

Establishing ourselves on the firm foundation of the finished work of Jesus Christ is the indispensable element we must have before we can start out and continue to live a successful life.

Second, in order that we may prosper in Christ, we should establish a clearly defined and desirable spiritual value system of material things. At best, material things are means we can use to make our life more comfortable, but they must not rule us.

There is a certain order in both the spiritual and the physical world. It is most important that man should obey God, who is the source of this order. Then, through the name and authority of Jesus Christ, we can have dominion over the world of evil spirits and over all the physical world.

However, many people live a life of bondage to their material gain. Though they live in affluence, they are not blessed in all things. Some people think that happiness is found only in material things or in their surroundings. That is wrong thinking. When we put God first in our lives, the material things we gain do not cause us to fall into bondage.

We must acknowledge the sovereignty of God over ourselves and the material world. We must also love God and our neighbors. Then, for the first time, we can have dominion over the material world. We should be blessed in everything once we have become Christians.

4

Be in Health

We are still in the house of threefold blessings. After we came in by the entrance hall of the house, we visited the first room where we learned it is God's will that our souls should prosper. Then we entered the second room where all things will go well with us. Now we are standing in front of the door to the third and last room where we will find that it is God's will that we have good health.

God desires that we may live in good health. Death, which all men fear today, was not God's plan for man from the start. When God made man, He created him to live forever. Man was originally destined to walk with God forever in the garden of Eden, enjoying the fruit of the tree of life. The fall of man brought death upon himself and enslavement by sickness, the instrument of death. Man was now a mortal being. Consequently, in the cosmic plan of God to save man, deliverance from sickness was a part of His plan. God laid this responsibility upon His only begotten Son, Jesus. So strong was His divine will which cares for our health!

Let's open the door of the third room of His divine will and enter it. As we open the door, we see that God's desire for all of His people is good health! First, we should examine what prevents good health. What is the source of sickness? After that we will look into the modern church and the gift of divine healing. Then the only thing left for us to do is to go out of the room by the way in which our sickness is healed. Thus, when we go out of the room, we must have our new look! Our old appearance of sickness, curse and pain will be put off and taken away.

115

Source of Sickness

We must know what the source of sickness is in order that we may strengthen our weak bodies and regain health. Unless we know this, it is not possible to know deliverance from sickness. The nature and source of sickness do not want to be revealed, just as cancerous cells don't want to reveal their origin. Once the source of sickness is exposed to the cross of Christ it will immediately be broken down and killed, just as leprosy bacteria are killed immediately when exposed to the air.

The three evils which brought sickness to us are the devil, sin and the curse. Since these always operate and work together, they cannot be dealt with separately. The devil entices man to sin against God, and sin brings the curse of God. Now let's look at the powers of death which are the source of sickness.

Sin

The cause of spiritual death which came immediately to Adam and Eve was their sin: "And the Lord God commanded the man, saying, Of every tree of the garden thou mayest freely eat: But of the tree of knowledge of good and evil, thou shall not eat of it: for in the day that thou eatest thereof thou shalt surely die" (Gen. 2:16-17).

In spite of such a dreadful warning from God, Adam and Eve were deceived by Satan. So they ate the forbidden fruit, and they came under the judgment of death: "In the sweat of thy face shalt thou eat bread, till thou return unto the ground; for out of it wast thou taken: for dust thou art, and unto dust shalt thou return" (Gen. 3:19).

This was the beginning of human tragedy. Man died spiritually and his fellowship with God was severed. This death did not mean that man's existence ceased. This was "spiritual death." Man was consequently corrupted by the devil, the source of death. So God drove man out of the garden "lest he put forth his hand, and take also of the tree of life, and eat, and live forever" (Gen. 3:22). God banished Adam and Eve from the garden of Eden so that they and their descendants might not escape physical death forever. From that time the power of death began to work corruption in Adam's human spirit and to destroy his body: "Wherefore, as by one man sin entered into the world, and death by sin: and so death passed upon all men, for that all have sinned" (Rom. 5:13).

At the fall of man the death of the spirit, or the severance of dialogue with God, preceded the death of the body. We might say that the death of the spirit was the onset of death in general. A passage in the Book

116

of Job reads: "It shall devour the strength of his skin: even the firstborn of death shall devour his strength" (Job 18:13). This text refers to such death in symbolic terms.

The "firstborn of death" is the soul, which was dead as the price of sin, and the "strength of his skin" refers to our flesh. When Adam committed sin, his spirit died immediately and his body began to deteriorate. The human body was created so perfectly by God that it took almost 1,000 years after his spirit died for the power of death to destroy it.

Because the world is full of sin today, in fewer than 100 years the power of death has enough time to kill the body. This proves that man is bound by the power of sin and death.

Sin caused the death of the spirit, which resulted in the death of the body. The first stage of this process was sickness. Accordingly, the death of the spirit became the "firstborn of death."

Today, we should not seek treatment of sickness only for our physical needs. When we seek the *source* of the sickness and treat it, we can be treated more quickly and more perfectly. For this reason James exhorts us in his epistle, "Confess your faults one to another, and pray one for another, that ye may be healed" (James 5:16).

Here it is implied that sickness came into being because of sin. Therefore we must confess our sins before our sickness can be cured. Our cure is in the redeeming grace of Jesus, and we receive healing for the body as soon as our sins are forgiven.

The Devil

There is a dual relationship between sin and the devil. Wherever the devil is, there is always sin; wherever sin is, there is the devil. The devil tempts a man to commit sin by making him rebel against God. As its partner, sin brings sickness which destroys and corrupts human beings without ceasing.

"For the wages of sin is death" (Rom. 6:23). The devil has the power of death (Heb. 2:14) and unceasingly fuels sickness with his energy, continuously stealing, killing and destroying (John 10:10).

Consequently, the complete treatment of sickness is only possible when spiritual treatment is given before the physical treatment. It is the indwelling human spirit which gives life and energy to the human body so that it may function. If the spirit once leaves the body, even the strongest, toughest body will stop living and begin to decay. Luke notes in chapter 8 that when the daughter of Jairus, ruler of the synagogue, died, Jairus wanted Jesus to pray for her. When Jesus came to their home,

SALVATION, HEALTH & PROSPERITY

He took the dead child by the hand and said, "Maid, arise." Immediately the spirit of the child came back to her and she revived.

This is a good illustration that life is quickened when the spirit reenters the body. The fact that the spirit sustains the body is mentioned in several places of the Bible: "The spirit of a man will sustain his infirmity; but a wounded spirit who can bear?" (Prov. 18:14). "A merry heart doeth good like a medicine: but a broken spirit drieth the bones" (Prov. 17:22).

When man came into the power of death because of his sin, the devil began to attack his body, even to kill him. True physical health is obtained only after man's spirit is set free from the power of death and filled with the life of God.

Sickness refers to an organic state. It is a succession of effects resulting in the final destruction of physical life. The devil is the one behind the sickness and provides the destructive energy of the sickness. His work is to rob, kill and destroy. Consequently, if the devil departs from the sickness, the germs will decompose and disappear. There will be no one to feed the sickness or cause it to spread. The Bible teaches that "God anointed Jesus of Nazareth with the Holy Ghost and with power: who went about doing good, and healing all that were oppressed of the devil" (Acts 10:38).

Behind all the different kinds of diseases Jesus healed, the devil was always there providing the energy for the disease. When Jesus cast out the spirit of the devil, the strength of the disease was broken; the impaired body was restored to complete health. In the Bible many examples of diseases appear: "When the even was come, they brought unto Him many that were possessed with devils: and He cast out the spirits with His word" (Matt. 8:16). "When Jesus saw that the people came running together, he rebuked the foul spirit, saying unto him, Thou dumb and deaf spirit, I charge thee, come out of him, and enter no more into him" (Mark 9:25).

The devil and his myriads of demons bring all kinds of sicknesses and diseases. People may ask, "Aren't viruses the cause of disease?" I say again that Satan provides *all* elements, including viruses, with destructive energy. If anyone desires to be totally healed, he must first of all confess his sins and believe in Jesus who is the only One with the power to destroy sin and death. Sickness and disease are the weapons of the devil. The believer must receive the life-giving work of the Holy Spirit into his soul. The life of the Holy Spirit repels the works of the devil, who causes sickness and death. Then the devil departs. Not only is health restored, but the individual becomes healthier than he or she ever had been before.

The Curse

God is a righteous God. When man committed sin, he broke the direct commandment of God. Because He is righteous, God had to punish sin. The curse of sickness, death and pain are all results of disobeying God and becoming partners with the devil. Nevertheless, God prepared the way of salvation for us because He is not only the righteous God, but He is also the God of love and mercy. When people do not respond to His call and exhortation, God gives them up to their corrupted hearts so that they "receive in themselves that recompense of their error which was meet" (Rom. 1:27). This was the beginning of sickness which came to us as a curse. "Why should ye be stricken any more? ye will revolt more and more: the whole head is sick, and the whole heart faint. From the sole of the foot even unto the head there is no soundness in it; but wounds, and bruises, and putrifying sores: they have not been closed, neither bound up, neither mollified with ointment" (Is. 1:5-6).

Sickness usually comes as the curse of the law. It is the snare and torment of the devil who is trying to "rob, kill and destroy" (John 10:10). Satan is a tormentor. If God, in His tenderness and mercy, had not protected this world from the evil power of the devil, the world would already have perished. If God had not shown His goodness and waited for our return to Him in repentance, we would have been destroyed long ago like Sodom and Gomorrah.

Let us consider the curse of sickness which God permitted and sent because man disobeyed: "The Lord shall send upon thee cursing, vexation and rebuke, in all that thou settest thine hand unto for to do, until thou be destroyed, and until thou perish quickly, because of the wickedness of thy doings, whereby thou hast forsaken me. The Lord shall make the pestilence cleave unto thee, until he have consumed thee from off the land, whither thou goest to possess it. The land shall smite thee with a consumption, and with a fever, and with an inflammation, and with an extreme burning, and with the sword, and with blasting, and with mildew" (Deut. 28:20-22).

"The Lord will smite thee with the botch of Egypt, and with the emerods and with the scab, and with the itch, whereof thou canst not be healed. The Lord shall smite thee with madness, and blindness, and astonishment of heart" (Deut. 28:27-28). "The Lord shall smite thee in the knees, and in the legs, with a sore botch that cannot be healed, from the sole of thy foot unto the top of thy head" (Deut. 28:35). "Moreover he will bring upon thee all the diseases of Egypt, which thou wast afraid of; and they shall cleave unto thee. Also every sickness, and every plague, which is not written in the book of this law, them will the Lord bring upon thee, until thou be destroyed'' (Deut. 28:60-61).

What a dreadful and frightening curse this is! This is the curse of the law, which came upon those who lived according to their lust. Such a phenomenon is taking place before our eyes today. In spite of all the efforts to set man free from sickness and death, the number of patients in the hospitals today is increasing, and incurable diseases are increasing rather than diminishing.

By now the persons who are reading this book may be confused, for in the previous sections it has been maintained that the cause of sickness comes to us as the curse of sin and Satan, but in this section it is contended that sickness came to us as the curse of God because of men's willful disobedience of God's instructions. Of course sickness itself is caused by man's sin and is enhanced by the devil, to whom is given the power of death (Heb. 2:14). Man sinned and fell under the judgment of the curse, and he is given over to be oppressed by the devil through sickness and death.

The following is taken from Job 2:6-7: ''And the Lord said unto Satan, Behold, he is in thine hand....So Satan went forth from the presence of the Lord, and smote Job with sore boils from the sole of his foot unto his crown.''

Sickness came into the world when man was delivered into the hand of Satan, being cursed by the law for his sin. Today God passes judgment on the bodies of men who commit sin. Man is delivered into the hand of the devil and comes under the curse of sickness.

The apostle Paul wrote, ''For all have sinned and come short of the glory of God'' (Rom. 3:23). This scripture shows that all men are delivered into the hands of the devil and are under the curse of the law. This scripture also shows that medical treatment alone cannot conquer sickness, for even if you succeed in overcoming one disease, the devil inevitably will cause another incurable disease as long as sin is in the life. We must confess our sins and be cleansed and forgiven, before we can be free from sin and the curse of the devil. We need an omnipotent Sovereign who can deliver and redeem us from such a source of disease. He is our Lord Jesus Christ, who has truly become the good news for us. The Bible reads: ''Being justified freely by His grace through the redemption that is in Christ Jesus'' (Rom. 3:24). ''Christ hath redeemed us from the curse of the law, being made a curse for us: for it is written,

Cursed is every one that hangeth on a tree" (Gal. 3:13).

These scriptures of promise and grace bring home to us the amazing love of God. Our God is certainly the God of righteousness and judgment. He made man undergo the affliction of sickness, but He is the God of love and mercy as well. Out of such love He sent Jesus, upon whom He laid our disobedience and sins. Thus Christ came under the curse for us.

If anyone confesses his sins and believes in the precious blood and the power of the Lord Jesus, his sins are forgiven and he receives salvation. He is delivered from the curse of the law: "Who hath delivered us from the power of darkness, and hath translated us into the kingdom of his dear Son: In whom we have redemption through his blood, even the forgiveness of sins" (Col. 1:13-14).

If our sins are forgiven, we should also be delivered from the torment of sin and sickness of the body. So then, does the redeeming grace of Jesus Christ include or cover our sickness? Let us now consider that question.

Jesus Bore Our Sickness

Jesus and Divine Healing

More than twenty years ago I pioneered my church in a shabby tent at Pulkwang-dong right after I graduated from Bible school. In order to prepare myself to preside at a funeral service, I searched the entire Bible for sermons which Jesus gave at funerals. Though I searched through the Bible from the first page in Genesis to the last page of Revelation, I could not find one reference to a funeral service. Jesus gave a sermon on a mountain, including sayings which we call the Beatitudes. He also delivered His sermon on the sower at the shore of the Sea of Galilee. But He did not utter one funeral sermon. On the contrary, He stopped a funeral and raised the dead.

When the daughter of the ruler of the synagogue was dead, Jesus did not deliver a sermon. Instead, He said to the little girl, "Damsel, I say unto thee, arise" (Mark 5:41).

Furthermore, when Lazarus had been dead for four days, Jesus said, "Lazarus, come forth," and Lazarus came out, bound hand and foot with grave clothes (John 11:43-44).

These events convince us that Jesus Christ is the Lord of life, the One who overcame death and the grave and their power. We see that everywhere He went Jesus forgave sins and healed the sick. He gave life by raising the dead—not only those who were spiritually dead, but those who were physically dead as well.

Forgiveness of Sins and Healing

Forgiveness of sins and healing are two things Jesus did wherever He went. These were the important things in His ministry. In all places Jesus forgave sins and healed sickness. Two-thirds of His ministry was spent in healing. Wherever Jesus went, the sinners and the sick followed Him. They witnessed the miracles by which the sick were healed and raised from their beds.

One day when Jesus was preaching the gospel in a home in Capernaum, four men took the roof partly off the house and lowered a paralytic through the ceiling, wanting Jesus to pray for him. Jesus said to the paralyzed man, "Son, thy sins be forgiven thee."

Some scribes of the Jews became indignant and thought, Who can forgive sins except God? Jesus knew what they were thinking. So He said to them, "Whether it is easier to say to the sick of the palsy, Thy sins be forgiven thee: or to say, Arise, and take up thy bed and walk? But that ye may know that the Son of man hath power on earth to forgive sins" (Mark 2:9-10). And then Jesus told the man, "Arise, and take up thy bed, and go thy way into thine house" (verse 11).

When his sin was forgiven, his sickness was cured. Strictly speaking, those whose sins are forgiven should also be delivered from the bondage of sickness. Jesus explicitly said this on the subject: "Whosoever committeth sin is the servant of sin. And the servant abideth not in the house for ever: but the Son abideth ever. If the Son therefore shall make you free, ye shall be free indeed" (John 8:34-36).

In what way shall the Son make us free? The Son delivers man from the bondage of sin and sets him free from his sin and sicknesses which came as punishment of sin. Since Jesus was indeed God, He had the power to forgive sins. Ironically, this was proven by the critical question asked by the scribes. Jesus combined forgiveness and healing, showing that both were inseparable. Even the scribes who said, "Who is this that forgiveth sins also?" (Luke 7:49), could not find fault with Jesus when they saw the man arise, take up his bed and go home. The fact that Jesus had the authority to forgive sins could not have been better demonstrated than that.

When Jesus healed the sick, He forgave their sins and He gave them faith to believe they had been forgiven. Our Lord said to the man at the pool of Bethesda, "Sin no more, lest a worse thing come upon thee" (John 5:14).

122

And when a woman who was diseased with an issue of blood twelve years touched the hem of His garment, Jesus said, "Thy faith hath made thee whole" (Matt. 9:22).

Of course the Bible tells of sicknesses which are not caused by sin. The man who was blind from birth was such a case. Jesus said that the fact that he was born blind was neither because of his sin nor because of the sins of his parents; rather he was born blind so that the works of God could be shown in him. This means that a person's sickness is not necessarily caused by sin. But sickness came into being and reached all mankind because of the original sin of Adam and Eve, with whom we have joint responsibility. Therefore a man should first receive forgiveness of sins before he is healed of his illness.

The Bible shows that whenever Jesus forgave sins the devil was cast out: "God anointed Jesus of Nazareth with the Holy Ghost and with power: who went about doing good, and healing all that were oppressed of the devil; for God was with Him" (Acts 10:38).

When our Lord forgave sins and worked miracles, the unclean spirits, crying out with a loud voice, were driven out of many that were possessed with them; for at the moment when Jesus forgave the sins of the sick, the devil lost the basis on which he could keep them as servants in his bondage. The fact that we have been delivered from sickness attests to the other fact that we have been set free from the bondage of the devil.

Jesus was referring to the Jubilee of the Old Testament when He said in Luke 4:19: "To preach the acceptable year of the Lord." The Jubilee is a clear picture of the blessing we are to receive in the dispensation of grace. When we look at Leviticus 25:8-12, we see that prior to the announcement of the year of Jubilee, there was a day of atonement. On the day of atonement a sacrificial animal was killed, and its blood was sprinkled on the mercy seat so that the sins of the people might be forgiven. Following this the Jubilee trumpet was sounded. Then the people who had lost their land or their homes for a long time received them back, and those who had been sold into bondage in exchange for their debts were forgiven and restored to their families.

This symbolizes the fact that the mercy and blessing of God come to us only through the redemption of Christ's cross. Jesus became our sin offering when He was crucified on the cross at Calvary and sprinkled His blood on the mercy seat of heaven. Thus, with His blood Jesus restored all things we had lost. By sending the Holy Spirit to us, He blew the joyful trumpet of the gospel and proclaimed our liberation from the devil.

After the trumpet was sounded in the year of Jubilee, God commanded the people of Israel, saying, "Proclaim liberty throughout all the land unto all the inhabitants thereof...And ye shall return every man unto his possessions" (Lev. 25:10).

Because we are the people of Christ, the One who offered a more excellent sacrifice under a better covenant, how much more necessary it is that our sins should be forgiven and that we should be set free from the power of the devil.

Moreover, when Jesus forgave our sins and healed the sick, what He had done became the very proof that He had set us free from the curse of the law, since the source of our sickness originated in that curse caused by sin: "Christ hath redeemed us from the curse of the law, being made a curse for us: for it is written, Cursed is every one that hangeth on a tree" (Gal. 3:13).

Jesus was hung on the cross to redeem us from the curse; by doing so He set us free from all sickness.

Therefore, as sin joined hands with sickness in destroying man when Adam fell, so forgiveness joined hands with healing in restoring man, following the redeeming grace and saving power of Jesus Christ. They acted in concert to give man eternal life. Forgiveness and healing were inseparable companions in the ministry of Jesus. When Jesus sent His disciples, He commanded them to heal the sick as well as to proclaim forgiveness. This is the Great Commission of the Lord, which has not changed.

"And when he had called unto him his twelve disciples, he gave them power against unclean spirits, to cast them out, and to heal all manner of sickness and all manner of disease" (Matt. 10:1).

Why Did Jesus Heal Sickness?

As we have seen, two thirds of the public ministry of Jesus was spent in healing the sick. Why did Jesus feel that healing was so important?

First, Jesus wanted to show that He was the Messiah, through His signs and wonders of divine healing. Jesus told this to those who accused Him when they denied that He was the Christ who came from God: "If I do not the works of my Father, believe me not. But if I do, though ye believe not me, believe the works: that ye may know, and believe, that the Father is in me, and I am in him" (John 10:37-38).

In this scripture Jesus emphatically testified that healing was the work of God and that He who carried out that work was the Messiah. Jesus also told these things to John the Baptist. At that time John the Baptist was in prison by the order of King Herod. John had testified that Jesus was the Lamb of God, but when he saw that Jesus was not promptly setting Israel free from Roman rule, he was disappointed and became doubtful. For that reason he sent his disciples to Jesus, asking Him, "Art thou he that is to come? or look we for another?" (Luke 7:20).

Then Jesus told John's disciples that He had healed many infirmities and sicknesses, had cast out many evil spirits and had given sight to the blind. Then He said: "Go your way, and tell John what things ye have seen and heard; how that the blind see, the lame walk, the lepers are cleansed, the deaf hear, the dead are raised, and to the poor the gospel is preached" (Luke 7:22).

John the Baptist had anticipated a political Messiah, but Jesus showed and proved Himself to be the Messiah who liberated people from the shackles of the devil. Those shackles were stronger and more burdensome than the shackles of the Roman government. Accordingly, if we believe that Jesus is the Messiah and Savior, we must also believe and experience His healing.

Second, healing is the manifestation of the grace and mercy of Jesus. In Psalm 145:8 David said, "The Lord is gracious, and full of compassion; slow to anger, and of great mercy." While Jesus Christ, the second person of the Trinity, was on earth in the flesh, He had compassion on those who were afflicted with sickness and demons. He healed the sick and cast demons out of those who were possessed: "And Jesus, moved with compassion, put forth His hand, and touched him, and saith unto him, I will; be thou clean" (Mark 1:41).

In spite of the threats of the religious leaders of the Jews who were breathing out death on the charge that He had broken the sacred Mosaic law on the Sabbath, Jesus still compassionately performed miracles and healed the sick. Even on the Sabbath Jesus cured "a woman which had a spirit of infirmity eighteen years, and was bowed together, and could in no wise lift up herself." He set her free from the sickness (Luke 13:11-12). Then the ruler of the synagogue rebuked the people with indignation saying, "There are six days in which men ought to work. In them therefore come and be healed, and not on the sabbath day."

Jesus answered him and said: "Thou hypocrite, doth not each one of you on the sabbath loose his ox or his ass from the stall, and lead him away to watering? And ought not this woman, being a daughter of Abraham, whom Satan hath bound, lo these eighteen years, be loosed from this bond on the sabbath day?" (Luke 13:15-16).

Thus Jesus healed the sick with tenderness and compassion wherever He went. Tenderness and mercy are the attitude of love. The Bible says, "God is love" (1 John 4:16). Because of this love, God the Son was incarnate in human flesh and came to this world. He forgave our sins and healed our sicknesses. Finally, He was crucified on the cross as a sin offering, to atone for our sins. He is our merciful and faithful high priest and is still interceding on our behalf. The Bible thus exhorts us: "For we have not an high priest which cannot be touched with the feeling of our infirmities; but was in all points tempted like as we are, yet without sin. Let us therefore come boldly unto the throne of grace, that we may obtain mercy, and find grace to help in time of need" (Heb. 4:15-16).

Because of this mercy and compassion, as many as are sick can come to our high priest, Jesus Christ, and obtain remission of their sins through the merits of His blood. They can also receive the healing of their sicknesses as well. Unless we expect the work of divine healing, we are denying that Jesus is our Savior and we are turning our faces from His divine love.

Redemption in the Old Testament

The major premise of the threefold blessings, the main subject of this book, is the cross of Jesus. This premise can be described thus: Man committed sin by rebelling against God. His spirit, soul and body were in bondage to Satan. But through the merits of the blood of Jesus which was shed on the cross, man was set free from the bondage of sin and death.

In view of this premise, sickness, which came upon man as the consequence of sin, must be included in the redeeming grace of the cross. If this grace had not been included in the redeeming work at the cross, however wonderful and full of tenderness and compassion Jesus' healing of the sick may have been, and though He spent two-thirds of His public ministry in this work, it would have ended merely as the compassion and work of a certain period. The New Covenant which was made between God and man can take eternal effect only through the cross.

Is it then certain that redemption from sickness through the cross was a grace of salvation God prepared before the world existed? If it is true that healing of sickness plays an important role in God's eternal work of salvation, we should be able to find that such healing was already prophesied or typified in the Old Testament. After all, the Old Testament is the show of the New Testament. Let us look into redemption from sickness in the types appearing in the Old Testament.

Passover Lamb

The Passover lamb is one of the important types which show the fact that redemption from sickness is included in Christ's work at the cross. In the first chapter of this book we saw that the Passover lamb symbolized Jesus Christ. The fact that the Israelites could be exempt from the plague of the death angel by putting the blood of the lamb on the doorposts shows that our sins have been forgiven through the blood of the lamb of God, Jesus Christ, and our souls are delivered from the wrath of judgment. Then what does the flesh of the lamb mean?

It is written in Exodus 12:46 and Numbers 9:12 that the children of Israel must eat the flesh of a lamb on the night of the Passover and leave none of it until morning. Also, they must break none of its bones. Thus the Bible links the body of the crucified Son of God with the flesh of the Passover lamb. Remember that the Roman soldiers broke the legs of the thieves on the other two crosses because they were not yet dead, but the soldiers did not break Jesus' legs because He was already dead (John 19:32-33).

The flesh of the Passover lamb provided health and strength for the children of Israel who had to take a long journey at night. Likewise, Jesus provided us with the power to be healed, as well as His strength for our long journey through life until He returns for His people. The prophet Isaiah recorded the Word of the Holy Spirit: "With His stripes we are healed" (Is. 53:5).

The apostle Peter also testified boldly, inspired by the Spirit of revelation:

"Who his own self bare our sins in his own body on the tree, that we, being dead to sins, should live unto righteousness: by whose stripes ye were healed" (1 Pet. 2:24).

The feast of the Passover in the Old Testament includes in its symbolism the grace of the atonement which redeemed us from our sicknesses—by the stripes that were inflicted on Jesus' back.

Waters of Marah

When Moses entered the region of Marah in the desert of Shur, the sun was hot and the heat of the desert country made the people very thirsty. But the only water they could find was the bitter waters at Marah. The people complained to Moses about their thirst. Moses fell on his face before God who showed him a tree. When Moses threw the tree in the water, as God told him, the water became sweet and the people drank it.

This incident is a type which shows that the redeeming grace of God

127

which delivers us from sickness is included in Christ's work at the cross. The Old Testament is the shadow and type of the New Testament. Moses, who led the people of Israel out of Egypt, delivered them from the bondage of the Egyptians and went with them through the wilderness toward the land of Canaan, is another type of Jesus. Christ, the great deliverer, calls His people out of a sinful world to lead them to the new heaven and the new earth.

The bitter waters of Marah signify the trouble and sickness which our spirits and bodies go through on our journey through life, and the tree which was cast into the water signifies the cross of Jesus Christ. In this very place God made a covenant of healing with the people of Israel: "There he made for them a statute and an ordinance, and there he proved them, and said, If thou wilt diligently hearken to the voice of the Lord thy God, and wilt do that which is right in his sight, and will give ear to his commandments, and keep all his statutes, I will put none of these diseases upon thee, which I have brought upon the Egyptians: for I am the Lord that healeth thee" (Ex. 15:25-26).

In this scripture the original Hebrew word for "the Lord that healeth" is *Yahweh Rophekah*. This holy name of the everlasting God explicitly shows that it is not God's will to cause sickness but to cure it. Nor is it His will to inflict death on man, but to give life.

Through the incident of making the bitter waters of Marah sweet, God made two million people of Israel depend on the God who heals. They lived in a wilderness where there were no sanitary facilities, and things such as food, clothing and shelter were in a very poor condition. Actually, if God had not healed them and bound up their wounds, countless numbers of the people would have fallen sick and died in the middle of the journey.

All of the Israelites, however, believed in the words of promise from God and obeyed Him; and they were all healed of their sicknesses. Among them there were neither weak nor sick people throughout the whole journey. Inspired by the Holy Spirit the psalmist wrote the following words, looking back upon those days: "He brought them forth also with silver and gold: and there was not one feeble person among their tribes" (Ps. 105:37).

The Israelites who were freed from bondage in Egypt are a good type of today's Christians who have been set free from the life of sin. The crossing of the Red Sea is a beautiful parallel of the regeneration of believers. The Israelites' life in the wilderness symbolizes our life on earth, as pilgrims and strangers, until we reach our heavenly land of promise.

Therefore, the healing of sicknesses, both spiritual and physical, should necessarily be our experience because we are under "a better covenant, which was established upon better promises" (Heb. 8:6). We follow in the footsteps of Jesus who is "surety of a better testament" (Heb. 7:22). That promise is written in Mark 16:17-18: "And these signs shall follow them that believe; in my name shall they cast out devils...they shall lay hands on the sick, and they shall recover."

The covenant of healing that was made at Marah was a type, showing that the grace of healing is included in the redemption of the cross. The covenant of healing was finally confirmed by Christ at the cross. Now we can live in good health until we enter that world where "there shall be no more death, neither sorrow, nor crying, neither shall there be any more pain" (Rev. 21:4).

The Bronze Serpent

"And they journeyed from Mount Hor by the way of the Red Sea, to compass the land Edom: and the soul of the people was much discouraged because of the way. And the people spake against God, and against Moses, Wherefore have ye brought us up out of Egypt to die in the wilderness? for there is no bread, neither is there any water; and our soul loatheth this light bread. And the Lord sent fiery serpents among the people, and they bit the people; and much people of Israel died. Therefore the people came to Moses and said, We have sinned, for we have spoken against the Lord, and against thee; pray unto the Lord, that he take away the serpents from us. And Moses prayed for the people. And the Lord said unto Moses, Make thee a fiery serpent, and set it upon a pole: and it shall come to pass, that every one that is bitten, when he looked upon it, shall live. And Moses made a serpent of brass and put it upon a pole, and it came to pass, that if a serpent had bitten any man, when he beheld the serpent of brass, he lived" (Num. 21:5-9).

This account of the bronze serpent also foreshadows Jesus' redemptive work of grace in delivering us from sickness through His crucifixion.

It may have been that there were many fiery serpents in that region, but the people of Israel were safe from the dangers of the serpents before this time because God had protected them with a strong arm. However, as soon as they rebelled against God and sinned, God's protection was lifted. Immediately the fiery serpents attacked and they bit and killed the people. These fiery serpents symbolize the devil, and this incident shows that when God's protection is lifted from believers, the devil always attacks them as a lion attacks his prey.

God instructed Moses to make a brass serpent and set it on a pole, and anyone bitten by a fiery serpent was healed from the moment he looked at the brass serpent. When the people of Israel repented of their sins, God's protection returned to them. This story had a prophetic meaning: One day the devil, who had been constantly tormenting people, would be totally defeated. This prophecy literally came true through the life and work of Jesus Christ.

When Nicodemus, a ruler of the Jews, came to Jesus by night, Jesus said to him, "And as Moses lifted up the serpent in the wilderness, even so must the Son of Man be lifted up: that whosoever believeth in him should not perish, but have eternal life" (John 3:14-15).

The brazen serpent of Moses was a picture of Jesus' redemptive work which He would fulfill on the cross. The serpent of brass which Moses made was prophetic. Moses' placing it high upon a pole symbolized the complete defeat of our enemy, the devil, described as "that old serpent, called the Devil, and Satan" (Rev. 12:9). Thus the crucifixion of Jesus actually accomplished the complete defeat of our enemy, the devil. The Bible attests this fact: "And [Jesus] said unto them, I beheld Satan as lightning fall from heaven. Behold, I give unto you power to tread on serpents and scorpions, and over all the power of the enemy: and nothing shall by any means hurt you" (Luke 10:18-19). "Now is the judgment of this world: now shall the prince of this world be cast out" (John 12:31). "In my name shall they cast out devils" (Mark 16:17). "And having spoiled principalities and powers, he made a shew of them openly, triumphing over them in it" (Col. 2:15).

These "principalities and powers" are described in Ephesians 6:12. Therefore just as the poison of the fiery serpents was rendered useless when Moses lifted up the brazen serpent on the pole in the wilderness, so the forces of the devil were cut off once and for all by the redeeming death of our Lord Jesus Christ.

A powerful work of divine healing took place and saved the lives of those who would otherwise have died, when the people of Israel looked at the brazen serpent which was lifted up on the pole. This was a type or shadow of the redemptive work of Jesus Christ who has the power to heal all people who turn to Him.

The great revivalist, F.F. Bosworth, who shook America and Canada with the mighty gift of divine healing, wrote as follows in his book *Christ the Healer: Message on Divine Healing*: "If healing was not to be in the atonement, why were these dying Israelites required to look at the type of the atonement for bodily healing? Since both healing and forgiveness came through the type of atonement, why not to us through Christ, the Antitype?''

We have seen the three types in the Old Testament which signify Jesus' redemption, the redemption of our sick bodies as well as our souls. Our Lord is God, the healer, who wants to heal our sicknesses. God wants us to be in good health. This is the good thinking of our good God.

Sickness came to us as punishment for sin committed at the fall of Adam and Eve. When Jesus rose again from the dead three days after He died on the cross, the devil was already bound. Then remission of sins and healing were given to as many as called on the name of Jesus Christ.

In order to explain this fact more clearly, we will now look closely at the gospel which the prophet Isaiah preached, for the life of Jesus Christ and His purpose are vividly prophesied in Isaiah 53.

Isaiah: The Gospel of Divine Healing

Isaiah was a prophet of God who lived in the land of Judah between 750 and 695 B.C. The book of Isaiah may be described as a book of the gospel in the Old Testament because it gives a detailed prophecy concerning our Lord Jesus on the cross, just as if the writer had seen the crucifixion. Careful reading of this chapter reveals the redeeming death of the Lord Jesus Christ in a most vivid way. By interpreting a few original Hebrew words appearing in Isaiah 53, we will see whether sickness is really included in the redemptive work of Jesus on the cross.

Choli: Sickness, Grief

The Hebrew word for sickness is the title for this section. Throughout the Old Testament *choli* means sickness, grief. "And the Lord will take away from thee all sickness [*choli*]" (Deut. 7:15). "Also every sickness [*choli*] and every plague" (Deut. 28:61).

In many other places of the Bible we find examples of the use of this word. In the King James Version, this same word *choli* is translated as "grief" or "griefs" in Isaiah 53:3-4. Accordingly, "acquainted with grief" in verse 3 means "acquainted with sickness," and "surely he hath borne our griefs" in verse 4 means "surely he hath borne our sicknesses." It means that Jesus knew our sicknesses and He bore them.

Makob: Suffering, Pain

This is the Hebrew word for suffering or pain: "But his flesh upon him shall have pain [*Makob*], and his soul within him shall mourn" (Job 14:22). "He is chastened also with pain [*Makob*] upon his bed, and the

131

multitude of his bones with strong pain" (Job 33:19).

This word is translated in the King James Version as "sorrows" (Is. 53:3-4). This tells us that the Hebrew word *Makob* means the sorrow arising from the pain of sickness. With this knowledge of the original language, we can read Isaiah 53:4 in this way: "Surely he hath borne our sickness [griefs] and carried our pain [sorrow caused by suffering]."

This verse literally means that our Lord Jesus, on our behalf, took upon Himself all of our sicknesses and suffered all kinds of pain, agony and sorrow coming from sicknesses. The fact that the original Hebrew testifies so prevents us from interpreting that verse in a different way, whether spiritually or symbolically. In addition there is a sure proof which makes the meaning of the scripture unequivocal. That is the word which the Holy Spirit inspired Matthew to quote in his gospel: "When the even was come, they brought unto him many that were possessed with devils: and he cast out the spirits with his word and healed all that were sick: that it might be fulfilled which was spoken by Esaias the prophet, saying, Himself took our infirmities, and bare our sicknesses" (Matt. 8:16-17).

That latter part is quoted from Isaiah 53:4 in an explanatory way by the Holy Spirit. In this quotation the Holy Spirit clearly shows us that divine healing comes from the redemption of the cross. Therefore, no one could refute the truth that Jesus also redeemed us from our sicknesses and pains in His work of redemption.

Sabal: Bear, Carry Away

Through the Hebrew word *sabal* we can know that sin and sickness were included together in being "carried away": "He shall see of the travail of his soul, and shall be satisfied: by his knowledge shall my righteous servant justify many; for he shall bear [*sabal*] their iniquities" (Is. 53:11).

"Surely he hath borne our griefs, and carried [*sabal*] our sorrows" (Is. 53.4).

The word *sabal* in these two verses testifies that Jesus carried our pain and suffering coming from sickness, as well as bore our sins. Accordingly, if we believe that Christ redeemed us from our sins, we should believe that He redeemed us from our sicknesses also. If we cannot believe in *both* kinds of redemption, we must not believe in *any* kind of redemption, for Jesus carried away both our sins and our sicknesses. If it is true that Jesus took our sins and bore our iniquities, it must also be true that He carried away our sickness and our pain. If we have freely received remission of sins, we must also freely receive healing through faith. This is a truth which we can neither deny nor change, for it is clear in God's Word.

The Hebrew word *sabal* signifies the figure of a woman with child dragging herself away with a groan. This tells us that Jesus, like a woman with child, hung on a cross bearing our sins and sickness. He was giving birth to redemption and healing in the agony of those last painful hours.

Nasa: Bore

In Isaiah 54 there is another word which shows that Jesus bore our sins and sickness at the same time and redeemed us from them both. That is the Hebrew word *nasa*.

"And He bare (*nasa*) the sin of many" (Is. 53:12). "Surely he hath borne [*nasa*] our griefs [sicknesses]" (Is. 53:4).

As we can see in these two verses, the same Hebrew word *nasa* in the context meant both to bear sins and to bear sickness. Its meaning is to lift up, carry away or remove far away. This same word is used in Leviticus 16, when describing the scapegoat which went away into an uninhabited land, carrying all the iniquities of the Israelites. "And Aaron shall lay both his hands upon the head of the live goat, and confess over him all the iniquities of the children of Israel, and all their transgressions in all their sins, putting them upon the head of the goat, and shall send him away by the hand of a fit man into the wilderness: And the goat shall bear [*nasa*] upon him all their iniquities unto a land not inhabited: and he shall let go the goat in the wilderness" (Lev. 16:21-22).

On the day of atonement the people of Israel brought two goats. They killed one to atone for all the sins of Israel, and they sprinkled its blood on the altar. But they sent the other one away for a scapegoat into the wilderness. This scapegoat was to wander endlessly in the wilderness, bearing the countless sins of the children of Israel until it finally fainted and perished.

The scapegoat also typifies our Lord Jesus. As the scapegoat went into the wilderness bearing all the sins of the Israelites, so Jesus died on the cross bearing all our sins and paying the price of our sins once for all. This aspect of the gospel of divine healing is straightforwardly described in Isaiah 53:5: "But he was wounded for our transgressions, he was bruised for our iniquities: the chastisement of our peace was upon him; and with his stripes we are healed."

Quoting this scripture, Peter writes eloquently that our Lord redeemed us from our sins and sicknesses at the same time: "Who his own self bare our sins in his own body on the tree, that we, being dead to sins, should live unto righteousness: by whose stripes ye were healed'' (1 Pet. 2:24).

Our Comforter, the Holy Spirit, clearly emphasizes this truth by saying, ''...ye were healed'' (past tense). The price of our sins and sickness was paid completely 2,000 years ago on the cross. What remains is for us to believe firmly this accomplished fact and appropriate it.

God earnestly desires that we should be delivered from our sicknesses. Isaiah clearly shows this desire of God: ''Yet it pleased the Lord to bruise him; he hath put him to grief'' (Is. 53:10).

Why did God want His only Son, Jesus Christ, to undergo the suffering of the stripes and the cross? It was because God wanted to deliver us from grief. Why was Jesus silent, not opening His mouth, and afflicted to the very last like a speechless lamb before her shearers? It was because He willingly set out to redeem us from our sorrow and pain.

Therefore, if Christians profess that their sins are forgiven, but do not want to be redeemed from sickness and pain, this becomes itself a grave sin which is committed against the will of God. It makes the redemption plan for their lives incomplete. There are actually many Christians who have such half-way faith. Since God already foreknew that there would be such people, He deplored this fact through Isaiah's writing, saying, ''Who hath believed our report?'' (Is. 53:1). Through the study of Isaiah 53 we have reached the conclusion that the gospel includes divine healing also. God wants to deliver us from sickness and pain. We will now see how the modern church understands and accepts the gifts of divine healing.

The Modern Church and Divine Healing

As previously mentioned, the church teaches healing as one of the three rites of the holy sacrament, together with baptism and communion, and believes that they should be kept until the end of time. Nevertheless, modern churches have changed this sacrament. In some churches baptism has been changed to the rite of sprinkling upon the recipient's head. So far, the communion service in the modern church is still kept, but in some churches it is observed only once or twice a year. As for healing, most churches have totally omitted it. Such a state shows point-blank that the modern church is a long way from the Word of God.

Was the gift of divine healing really given to the church? If it was, is it still in effect today? Does the Holy Spirit still continue His work of healing?

134

The Gifts of Divine Healing Are Appointed by God

"And God hath set some in the church, first apostles, secondarily prophets, thirdly teachers, after that miracles, then gifts of healings" (1 Cor. 12:28).

Gifts of healing are included in the diverse gifts established by God for the church. This fact is affirmed by James: "Is any sick among you? let him call for the elders of the church; and let them pray over him, anointing him with oil in the name of the Lord: and the prayer of faith shall save the sick, and the Lord shall raise him up; and if he have committed sins, they shall be forgiven him" (Jas. 5:14-15).

James was the brother of Jesus and was leader of the Jerusalem church council (Acts 15:13). The apostle Paul said James was a pillar of the church (Gal. 2:9). When two factions formed as a result of different opinions on the issue of circumcision—one claiming that the Gentiles who were saved should keep the law and be circumcised, the other claiming that since they were saved by faith, they had no need of circumcision— James put an end to the argument by saying, "Wherefore my sentence is…" (Acts 15:19). This was the kind of authority James had among the apostles. The other disciples were silenced by his conclusion and obeyed him. Since his proclamation was written in the public letter which James wrote to all the church, we can accept the authority by which James wrote about the gifts of healing God had given to the church.

In addition, this epistle was written during the last days of the apostolic age when there were few apostles remaining. Most of the apostles had left this world. So the power of healing could not be entrusted solely to the hands of the apostles. The power of healing was given to other church leaders, namely the elders who were within easy reach of the congregation. Therefore the elders of the church have the biblical authority to receive and exercise this gift appointed by God as long as the church exists on the earth. The elders of the church in those days were the same as today's leaders of congregations—namely the clergy, pastors and licensed ministers, and those who are filled with the Holy Spirit and the Word.

We have thus seen in detail that the gift of divine healing is an authoritative gift appointed by God, and this gift operates through those ministering in the body of Christ. However, some may still have doubts about this, wondering, "Hasn't the gift of healing disappeared since the early church?" I would refer to the following scriptures in answering this question.

Jesus came to the synagogue in Nazareth on the Sabbath day and read this scripture in the book of the prophet Isaiah: "The Spirit of the Lord is upon me, because he hath anointed me to preach the gospel to the poor; he hath sent me to heal the brokenhearted, to preach deliverance to the captives, and recovering of sight to the blind, to set at liberty them that are bruised, to preach the acceptable year of the Lord" (Luke 4:18-19).

This scripture was actually fulfilled. Jesus not only set people free who were enslaved by sin, but He actually cast demons out of a man from Gergesa who was possessed by many demons, named Legion. In addition, Jesus not only opened the eyes of the spiritually blind. He actually gave sight to a man who had been blind from birth. He healed the blindness of Bartimaeus, the beggar. What do the words "To set at liberty them that are bruised" mean? We can find the answer in the sermon which Peter delivered at the house of Cornelius, a Gentile Christian: "How God anointed Jesus of Nazareth with the Holy Ghost and with power: who went about doing good, and healing all that were oppressed of the devil; for God was with him" (Acts 10:38).

Therefore, "to set at liberty them that are bruised" means to release people from the oppression of the devil. Jesus released all such people, including the sick. After Jesus read this scripture from the book of Isaiah, He said, "This day is this scripture fulfilled in your ears" (Luke 4:21).

Our Lord didn't say that this scripture would be fulfilled in the distant future, but emphasized that it had been fulfilled in that place. Our Lord desires that in this very hour the gift of healing may be poured out upon us abundantly. Jesus Christ wants to pour out this gift upon us so that the acceptable year of God may be preached today.

In the Old Testament the prophet Joel predicted that in the last days God would pour out His Spirit upon all flesh (Joel 2:28). The apostle Peter declared in his sermon, which he preached in the fullness of the Holy Spirit at Pentecost, that the "last days" referred to are the dispensation of grace, the time period we are living in (Acts 2:17). And James also spoke of "the early and the latter rain" (James 5:7). The Holy Spirit is pouring out this latter rain now. Can we deny the "manifestation of the Spirit" as mentioned in 1 Corinthians 12:7?

The manifestation of the Spirit includes "the gifts of healing" (1 Cor. 12:9), and these gifts are working by the absolute will of God (1 Cor. 12:11). Hence we are certain that the gift of healing has not disappeared, but that it will be manifested more and more among the churches of our time as the end of the age approaches.

Healing: the Foundation of the Kingdom of Heaven

When Jesus preached the gospel, demons were cast out and all kinds of sicknesses were healed. This brought ridicule from the Pharisees, who said, "This fellow doth not cast out devils, but by Beelzebub the prince of the devils" (Matt. 12:24). Then Jesus sternly rebuked them and declared, "But if I cast out devils by the Spirit of God, then the kingdom of God is come unto you" (Matt. 12:28).

By His Word Jesus showed that casting out demons and healing the sick are signs of the presence of the kingdom of heaven. Jesus is God and is living among us. When He is with us, the kingdom of heaven is with us, and divine healing is proof that this is so. Since the foundation of heaven is in healing, the Messiah who is the creator-builder of heaven must necessarily be the healer also. John the Baptist sent his disciples to Jesus to ask Him, "Art thou he that should come?" (Luke 7:19).

So Jesus answered thus: "Go your way and tell John what things ye have seen and heard: how the blind see, the lame walk, the lepers are cleansed, the deaf hear, the dead are raised, to the poor the gospel is preached" (Luke 7:22).

This passage states that the Messiah, who will deliver us from the agony of death and corruption, will be the healer. Jesus was the Great Physician who healed our spiritual sicknesses and revived our spirits. Why then could He not heal the sicknesses of our bodies which are inferior to the spirit?

In Malachi, the last book of the Old Testament, there is a wonderful prophecy concerning the Messiah as healer: "But unto you that fear my name shall the Sun of righteousness arise with healing in His wings; and ye shall go forth, and grow up as calves of the stall" (Mal. 4:2).

Since we have been healed from sickness of both spirit and body by Jesus the healer, we can live a healthy and dynamic life, like calves released from the stall. The reason why today's Christians are sick and feeble is that their sickness of spirit and body has not been healed. It is because the kingdom of heaven has not yet come upon their spirits and bodies. Preaching of the gospel produces the presence of the kingdom of heaven. The work of healing which comes as a result of gospel preaching is proof that the kingdom of heaven has already come.

Therefore, when Jesus appointed the 70 messengers and sent them out to preach the gospel, He charged them saying, "And heal the sick that are therein, and say unto them, The kingdom of God is come nigh unto you" (Luke 10:9).

The meaning of this exhortation of Jesus was that the seventy, after they healed the sick, should make it understood to the people that the miracle of healing was proof of the presence of the kingdom of God. Jesus explained once again the relationship between healing and the presence of the kingdom of heaven when the seventy messengers returned.

"And the seventy returned again with joy, saying, Lord, even the devils are subject unto us through thy name. And He said unto them, I beheld Satan as lightning fall from heaven....Notwithstanding in this rejoice not, that the spirits are subject unto you; but rather rejoice because your names are written in heaven" (Luke 10:17-18,20).

Have you accepted Jesus Christ as your Savior? Then the kingdom of heaven has already come to you. Do you believe that the kingdom of heaven is already within you? Then the healing power of Christ will be manifested. He is the Sun of righteousness (Mal. 4:2) and the God who heals. He is the merciful Lord who suffered the stripes and was crucified to redeem you from sickness and pain.

The kingdom of heaven was first proclaimed by Jesus, then by His twelve disciples and later by the seventy disciples. Afterwards, it was declared by innumerable Christians who lived before us. Today more than 1.5 billion Christians all over the world are testifying to it. The power and work of healing should be overflowing today throughout His church and the whole world. Nevertheless, today's church is crowded with patients who are gravely ill in their spirits and bodies, because the church is not preaching the gospel of healing. How this grieves God!

We should stop disputing whether healing is necessary for the church today and begin receiving light on healing. Then we should become witnesses who are healed from the sicknesses of spirit and body. We should preach the good news that the kingdom of God has already come to this earth through Jesus Christ. We must cast out all the tormenting evil spirits and set free those who are oppressed by the devil, by helping them believe in and experience the grace of healing, which is an aspect of the heavenly kingdom. Just as the church that does not preach the kingdom of heaven is useless, so the gospel message that does not contain healing is a deformed gospel message. Today, Jesus still desires earnestly that we should participate in building the kingdom of heaven through the gift of healing.

The Work of the Holy Spirit, the Other Comforter

We have seen that Jesus Christ bore our sicknesses and that God appointed the gift of healing among us. We have also seen that healing is the foundation of the kingdom of heaven and becomes proof of the presence of that kingdom. Some who read this book may still be in doubt, however, and have questions like this: "Didn't Jesus, who cast out demons and abolished disease, rise from the dead and ascend into heaven 2,000 years ago? Jesus isn't seen by people today, so who is doing His work on earth now?"

We will now introduce the other Comforter, the Holy Spirit, to those who still have such questions. As we have seen in the first chapter of this book, our God is a good God. Therefore Jesus Christ, the second person of the Trinity, is also good. He wore the crown of thorns and was crucified. The third person of the Trinity is the Holy Spirit, and He is the good Holy Spirit who works out salvation, health and prosperity in our lives according to the directions of our good God.

Before His ascension Jesus gave us a wonderful and divine promise which no one had ever made before, and no other person will ever be able to make: "Go ye therefore, and teach all nations, baptizing them in the name of the Father, and of the Son, and of the Holy Ghost: teaching them to observe all things whatsoever I have commanded you: and, lo, I am with you alway, even unto the end of the world" (Matt. 28:19-20). "For where two or three are gathered together in my name, there am I in the midst of them" (Matt. 18:20).

Jesus was crucified. That was certain. He died and was placed in the tomb. With the same certainty we know that He arose from the dead and ascended into heaven. We cannot find His fleshly form on earth, and we cannot find the remains of His body. Jesus promised that He would be among us and with us. If Jesus is with us now, the same things which He did 2,000 years ago should appear daily in our lives. By this we can judge whether Jesus' sayings are true or not: If these things are not happening among us, the promise of Jesus has become empty words to us.

In what way, then, is Jesus here with us? Jesus said: "And I will pray the Father, and he shall give you another Comforter, that he may abide with you for ever; even the Spirit of truth; whom the world cannot receive, because it seeth him not, neither knoweth him: but ye know him; for he dwelleth with you, and shall be in you. I will not leave you comfortless: I will come to you" (John 14:16-18).

The Comforter signifies One who is sent to be an advocate for another and is always with that other. In this passage Jesus shows that He is the first Comforter. The Spirit of truth whom Jesus called "another Comforter" is *allos*, which means "one among two identical things."

Accordingly, Jesus and the Holy Spirit are both comforters. They are different from one another only in that the former came first and the latter followed Him.

The Holy Spirit who came down at Pentecost, after the resurrection and ascension of Jesus, did the work of Jesus in His name and in His place. So the Holy Spirit is another Comforter. Jesus certainly said, "I will not leave you comfortless: I will come to you" (John 14:18). This means that the presence of the Holy Spirit is the presence of Jesus. To make this point clearer, Jesus said, "At that day ye shall know that I am in my Father, and ye in me, and I in you" (John 14:20).

Jesus said that He would send the Holy Spirit to fill the vacancy made by His leaving and that He would be with us until the end of the world. What kind of work do you think the Holy Spirit did when He came? The Bible says, "Therefore being by the right hand of God exalted, and having received of the Father the promise of the Holy Ghost, he hath shed forth this, which ye now see and hear" (Acts 2:33).

What is "this, which ye now see and hear"? The Bible tells us: "He [the Holy Spirit] shall glorify me: for he shall receive of mine, and shall shew it unto you. All things that the Father hath are mine: therefore said I, that he shall take of mine, and shall shew it unto you" (John 16:14-15).

Through this saying Jesus clearly shows that "this, which ye now see and hear" is the work of salvation which He did in this world—forgiveness of sins and healing. This is the will and purpose of God our Father toward us. Through the verses of Isaiah quoted by Jesus we can see the work of Jesus which the Holy Spirit was doing: "The Spirit of the Lord is upon me, because he hath anointed me to preach the gospel to the poor; he hath sent me to heal the broken-hearted, to preach deliverance to the captives, and recovering of sight to the blind, to set at liberty them that are bruised, to preach the acceptable year of the Lord" (Luke 4:18-19).

These words are the proclamation of the gospel of Jesus Christ, and our Lord said that He would do this work through the anointing of the Holy Spirit. Now the same Holy Spirit has come to continue the same work in the church, the body of Christ. Even today the gospel is preached to the poor in spirit and in body. Deliverance is preached to the captives in sin, recovering of sight to the spiritually blind, healing to those who suffer from many sicknesses and are oppressed by the devil, and salvation to the whole world! Thus the other Comforter, the Holy Spirit Himself, is conferring the gifts of grace which Jesus Christ paid for through His suffering and death on the cross.

The Holy Spirit not only testifies of the grace of redemption Jesus wrought (John 15:26) and shows that grace to us (John 16:12-14), but by His unique ability to bring a spiritual revelation He helps us understand it (1 Cor. 12:3). He also makes it possible for that revelation to lead people into a born-again experience, which everyone who opens his heart can receive (Rom. 8:1-4). It should be clear that Jesus' healing is included in the above scriptures. The Bible certainly says, "To another the gift of healing by the same spirit" (1 Cor. 12:9). Notice that the phrase "gifts of healing" is plural.

The Holy Spirit, the other Comforter who dwells among us and continues Jesus' work, enables us to understand and receive forgiveness because of Jesus' work on Calvary. As an evidence that we have been forgiven, He heals us. Through the Holy Spirit we have the grace of salvation with healing as its sign. When we believe in Jesus, and when the Holy Spirit (the Comforter) is with us, the great works that Jesus performed 2,000 years ago should also be manifested among us.

The Idea That Healing Is Not Necessary

The redemption of Jesus Christ from sickness—His grace of healing—still continues in His church and it should. Nevertheless it is often said that healing is not necessary. Of course, such an idea may be the reflection of the confidence in the promotion of health which has been made possible by the advances in today's medical science and the improvements in our surroundings. Anyone, however, who has the eyes of faith can see sickness in the light of its connection with redemption from sin, can easily discern how worldly and sensual such an assertion is.

Since we receive salvation and the gifts of divine healing at the same time, we proclaim the truth that as many as are saved should also experience healing. The Bible shows us that all the disciples of Jesus taught this, laying the same emphasis upon salvation and divine healing. The evangelistic work of the apostle Peter centered on the salvation of souls and working miracles of divine healing as well as testifying (1 Pet. 2:24). "In so much as they brought forth the sick into the streets, and laid them on beds and couches, that at least the shadow of Peter passing by might overshadow some of them. There came also a multitude out of the cities round about unto Jerusalem, bringing sick folks, and them which were vexed with unclean spirits: and they were healed everyone" (Acts 5:15-16).

John the apostle, who leaned back on Jesus' breast at the Lord's supper, also spoke healing in the name of the Lord to a crippled beggar who was lying at the temple gate called Beautiful. And he wrote in his epistle, "I wish...that thou mayest prosper and be in health" (3 John 2).

The apostles of the early church regarded miracles of healing as equally important with the preaching of the gospel for the salvation of souls, and they prayed for miracles. In the very beginning of the Christian church, the apostles Peter and John were brought before the Sanhedrin to be questioned. But they were soon released, and they told the church what had happened in the meeting of the Sanhedrin. Then the church prayed thus: "And now, Lord, behold their threatenings: and grant unto thy servants, that with all boldness they may speak thy word, by stretching forth thine hand to heal; and that signs and wonders may be done by the name of thy holy child Jesus" (Acts 4:29-30).

God was well pleased with this prayer. As a sign, "the place was shaken where they were assembled together; and they were all filled with the Holy Ghost, and they spake the word of God with boldness" (Acts 4:31). The Bible further reads, "And with great power gave the apostles witness of the resurrection of the Lord Jesus: and great grace was upon them all" (Acts 4:33).

Today some people maintain that they should only preach the gospel. They not only regard it as a shameful thing that the Holy Spirit works signs and wonders while preaching the gospel, but they also criticize these works. Such false piety and legalism are hypocrisy, for he who preaches against such works neither goes into heaven himself nor permits others to enter.

Our gospel preaching must be in the power of the Holy Spirit, followed by signs and wonders; for wherever the gospel is preached the old man is thrown off and our old master, the devil, goes out with a loud cry. The apostle Paul, known as the apostle of apostles, took it for granted that the power of the Holy Spirit was manifested in preaching the gospel and professed that these things brought success to his preaching: "I have therefore whereof I may glory through Jesus Christ in those things which pertain to God. For I will not dare to speak of any of those things which Christ hath not wrought by me, to make the Gentiles obedient, by word and deed, through mighty signs and wonders, by the power of the Spirit of God; so that from Jerusalem, and round about unto Illyricum, I have fully preached the gospel of Christ" (Rom. 15:17-19).

Because we do not perform the things in our church which the apostle Paul performed, we fill the world inside and outside of our churches with civilized pagans.

If advanced science, philosophy and education of our present era are made more effective than these things that the apostle Paul performed, why are we unable to evangelize our society fully with philosophy and education? There are more pagans around us in our society than those who were in the time of the apostle Paul. How can we lead these pagans to obedience? Lest we deviate into a side path, Jesus entrusted us with the Great Commission, which could by no means be changed: "Go ye into all the world, and preach the gospel to every creature. He that believeth and is baptized shall be saved; but he that believeth not shall be damned. And these signs shall follow them that believe; in my name shall they cast out devils; they shall speak with new tongues; they shall take up serpents; and if they drink any deadly thing, it shall not hurt them; they shall lay hands on the sick, and they shall recover" (Mark 16:15-18).

This Great Commission is the will of God which cannot be changed. The attempt of our churches to keep signs, wonders and the power of the Holy Spirit at a distance and criticize them, was originally an attempt to cover up and justify the powerlessness of leadership. The result was that it grieved God and gratified the devil. Signs, wonders and the power of the Holy Spirit are essential for successful preaching of the gospel. "How shall we escape, if we neglect so great salvation; which at the first began to be spoken by the Lord, and was confirmed unto us by them that heard him; God also bearing them witness, both with signs and wonders, and with divers miracles, and gifts of the Holy Ghost, according to his own will?" (Heb. 2:3-4).

The gifts of healing should be used for the glory of God, since God ordained and appointed them in the church by using them Himself. Of course it is deplorable that these precious gifts have been misused and misapplied. Wherever we see the good work of God, however, there will always be interference of the devil, who transforms himself "into an angel of light" (2 Cor. 11:14).

We must disclose the true character of the devil by earnestly contending for the faith that was once delivered to the saints (Jude 3). We must show the power of the gospel to the whole world, by establishing the truth by the Word. By doing so we can prevent our vulnerable, thirsty flocks from secretly following after heretics and occultists who are going about in sheep's clothing but are inspired by the devil. We will be able to lead them away from error to the right path.

Let us open our hearts to the kingdom of God and allow these truths to come alive in ourselves and in our homes through healing in Christ.

Let us allow our sick bodies to experience the miraculous healing power of the other Comforter, the Holy Spirit, who even now comes bestowing upon us the same healing power that Christ had. Let us accept the gospel of salvation and healing, lest the pain of those stripes He suffered on our behalf be in vain.

"And the very God of peace sanctify you wholly; and I pray God your whole spirit and soul and body be preserved blameless unto the coming of our Lord Jesus Christ" (1 Thess. 5:23).

How Can Our Sicknesses Be Healed?

So far we have seen that the redemption of Jesus Christ includes redemption from our sicknesses, and even today the healing power of Christ Jesus is being manifested in our bodies through that other Comforter, the Holy Spirit. This truth is as immovable as heaven and earth. Nevertheless vast numbers of Christians are still in agony, bound by sickness in their bodies. If we are saved by believing in Jesus, healing should follow as a result. Why then are so many children of God, who have confessed Jesus as Savior, still bound by this torment, the consequence of sin?

God must feel frustrated and hurt when He sees us bound and tormented in spite of being forgiven of our sins, because we refuse to receive the blessings He has prepared for us. Even though the refreshing rain from heaven is falling in abundance, we cannot receive it if our vessel is covered. In the same way, if we want to be set free from sin and its torments and enter into the blessings of heaven which have been prepared for our enjoyment, we must prepare our vessel to receive the blessing. We can prepare our vessel by taking the lid off, and the blessing of God will come to us in great showers, breaking any bondage of sickness, removing the agony. Then we will be delivered from sickness and live in health until we are called home to be with God forever. I would like to show you how to prepare your vessel to contain this blessing of health.

Eagerly Desire Health

Like any other blessing, healing comes to those who yearn for it. God cannot give gifts to people who are indifferent or who are not sure if they should accept the gifts. Those who want to be delivered from the power of sickness should have a strong desire for perfect health. They should yearn for it.

Jesus met with a man who had been sick for 38 years at the Pool of Bethesda. He had been waiting at the pool every day for an opportunity to step into the water first after it had been stirred by an angel, but his weakness was so severe that he could not get in before others. Jesus asked him the strange question, "Wilt thou be made whole?" (John 5:6). Jesus was asking whether the man was really ready to be healed, whether he earnestly desired healing.

Everyone makes various decisions in daily life. These decisions lead us either to good or bad. If a patient makes up his mind that he wants to be healed, the medicine he takes will take quick effect, and the cure will be effective. If the patient decides that he will always be sick and looks for the approach of death, no medicine can help him.

Actually, some sick people do not want to be healed, because when they are sick they receive a lot of attention. Their families and friends have compassion on them and pamper them. There are others who are sick because they desire to go to be with the Lord. If they are sick because they have no will to survive in this world, no one can blame them.

Sick people must first of all have their hearts ready before they receive healing. God can never help us unless we really want His help.

After giving the parable of the unjust judge and the widow, Jesus said: "Hear what the unjust judge saith. And shall not God avenge his own elect, which cry day and night unto him, though he bear long with them?" (Luke 18:6-7).

This means that if we do not have a fervent desire to be healed or receive an answer from God, He cannot answer our prayer; but if it is a burning desire, God will satisfy that desire if it is not against His will. The Bible tells us this concerning our desires and their fulfillment: "Delight thyself also in the Lord; and he shall give thee the desires of thine heart" (Ps. 37:4). "For it is God which worketh in you both to will and to do of his good pleasure" (Phil. 2:13). Also, "...the desire of the righteous shall be granted" (Prov. 10:24).

Naaman, commander of the army of the king of Syria (2 Kin. 5:1-14), had honor, wealth and position, but he was a leper. His future was very dark. His heart burned with desire to be healed and delivered from his sickness. So he didn't reject the advice of a little slave girl.

When the slave girl told him that a prophet of Israel could heal his leprosy, he immediately prepared for the journey and traveled to Israel. Since Syria was at odds with Israel in those days, there was the strong possibility that he could be killed or taken captive; but his fervent desire to be healed from his affliction drove him to risk his life and visit Elisha.

When Elisha told him to bathe seven times in the Jordan River, Naaman came close to giving up the idea of being healed. But he accepted the advice of his servants and friends. He went into the muddy water and dipped seven times. He had to give up his pride. He had to obey the command of God's servant. At first he really thought he was too good to walk into that dirty water, but his desire to be healed was so strong that he did it anyway. The result was that his flesh became clear again like that of a child.

When Jesus preached in His hometown, He rebuked the people of Nazareth for their unbelief: "And many lepers were in Israel in the time of Eliseus the prophet; and one of them was cleansed, saving Naaman the Syrian" (Luke 4:27).

The woman mentioned in Mark 5:25-34, who had an issue of blood for twelve long years, was also healed because she had a strong desire to be healed. She had been reduced to skin and bone. She had visited many physicians, but they could not help her. As she went from one physician to another, she spent all the money she had. Since an issue of blood was an unclean disease, like leprosy, she had to suffer the spiritual agony as well as the physical pain. She was forced to be confined to a back room or a miserable hut away from her friends and family, and her condition became worse as time went by. Nevertheless, she had a strong desire for life and health.

Her eager desire enabled her to catch the news which might have passed unnoticed. In spite of the rebuke of the people, she went where Jesus was so that she might touch the hem of His garment. No one had told her that if she could just touch His clothes she would be healed. Thousands of people brushed past Jesus every day, pushing this way and that way, touching Him as they tried to get near Him. Nothing happened to them. But the woman had a personal revelation: "If I can only touch the hem of His garment...I shall be whole." It was a burning desire which caused her to keep trying until she actually touched His garment. Her great desire gave birth to faith. When she acted in faith, Jesus knew that virtue had gone out of Him.

If we want to be healed, we must have a longing and a burning desire for health, as well as the determination to press in closer to Jesus to receive deliverance from the sickness. Once we enter this stage, healing is one step closer.

Repent

When we believe in Jesus as our Savior and confess Him with our mouths, we are born of water and of the Holy Spirit. That action brings about a change in the whole person. Through this change we are delivered from the bondage of Satan and become children of God. But Satan goes about as a roaring lion, and he is always watching for an opportunity to regain his power over us. The devil is the same evil being who tempted Judas Iscariot to betray Jesus for money and incited Peter to interfere with Jesus' work of redemption. The devil is still working today.

If a believer goes against the leading of the Holy Spirit in his life, and the Holy Spirit removes His presence, the flesh takes control again, and Satan immediately takes possession of many areas of his life: "And even as they did not like to retain God in their knowledge, God gave them over to a reprobate mind, to do those things which are not convenient; being filled with all unrighteousness, fornication, wickedness, covetousness, maliciousness: full of envy, murder, debate, deceit, malignity; whisperers, backbiters, haters of God, despiteful, proud, boasters, inventors of evil things, disobedient to parents, without understanding, covenantbreakers, without natural affection, implacable, unmerciful: who knowing the judgment of God, that they which commit such things are worthy of death, not only do the same, but have pleasure in them that do them" (Rom. 1:28-32).

If the devil is permitted to sow his seeds in our minds, soon our thinking will be controlled and manipulated by him. It cannot be emphasized too strongly that he is out to rob, kill or destroy all of God's people in any way he can. When he is permitted to reign unchecked long enough in our thoughts, attitudes or way of life, he will begin to sow disease until it slowly kills the spirit and then the body. We must rid ourselves of Satan's power, sanctifying ourselves through reading the Word (for the Word always sanctifies us), praying prayers of repentance and obeying the Word until we reach the place of full deliverance from sickness (1 Tim. 4:5; Eph. 5:26).

The Greek word for "repentance" is *metanoia*, which means a change in one's thinking. If we confess our sins and renew our minds with the Word so that our minds are subject to God instead of Satan, the devil will no longer rule our thought life. Then sickness which he brought will lose its power and die. When the devil departs, the virus which is the cause of all sickness and disease will lose its power. He will not be there to feed it or keep it alive. And when the devil has departed, new tissues or life will begin to replace the diseased area because Jesus came to give life and that more abundantly! The following scriptures will help us: "Keep thy heart with all diligence: for out of it are the issues of life" (Prov. 4:23). "Confess your faults one to another, and pray one for another, that ye may be healed'' (James 5:16).

Jesus always healed the sick and forgave sins at the same time. In my own ministry, when I prayed for people to be healed, I saw many people healed at the same time they were born again. When we repent of our sins, the devil gets frightened because he has lost his territory in our lives. So he quickly departs. God grants permanent healing only to those who confess their sins, make up their minds to live a God-centered life, and renew their minds in line with the Word of God.

Forgiveness

Forgiveness is the well from which healing flows to make our spirits and bodies whole. When Jesus said, ''Man, thy sins are forgiven'' (Luke 5:20), the man who was sick with palsy immediately rose up and walked. If we are to be healed by the power and authority of Jesus, we must first confess our sins and ask forgiveness.

When we are sick, our sins must first be forgiven in order that we may have the peace of mind that forgiveness brings. Even after we have been assured of forgiveness, the devil will accuse us, digging up our past mistakes and faults. So when we confess our sins, we must ask Jesus to help us remember everything we have done—our words, behavior and thinking—so that we may confess all of our sins, however great or small. This includes the sins of grieving God, causing damage to our neighbors, causing damage to friends or family, and anything which the Holy Spirit brings to our minds. We must be forgiven of all our sins and have the firm conviction that we are forgiven.

The devil always tries to suggest guilt to our hearts. If we are duped or confused by the whisperings of Satan, and fall prey to a guilty conscience, fear will follow. That fear will bring torment and our bodies will then become sick. The Holy Spirit can give us a firm conviction that our sins are forgiven. Then we will also be able to forgive ourselves and be free from the accusations of the devil. When we have received that assurance, we should not waver in our faith that God has forgiven. He takes pleasure in forgiving us when we repent. ''Come now, and let us reason together, saith the Lord: though your sins be as scarlet, they shall be as white as snow: though they be red like crimson, they shall be as wool'' (Is. 1:18).

Is forgiveness of our sins given to us at no cost? No, far from it. Since God is the God of righteousness, He was the One who determined what price He would require for sin. The great flood in Noah's time and the destruction of Sodom and Gomorrah attest to that. How can the righteous

God forgive our sins? He can forgive sin because He required the death of a sinless One to pay for sin. So Jesus hung on the cross and fully paid the price of all our sins. The precious blood of Jesus, full of power and authority to cleanse sin, is the only guarantee of His forgiveness. This guarantee can never be exhausted. So we can be forgiven if we only confess our sins to Jesus and believe that His blood has the power to cleanse them.

Through forgiveness of sins we can be delivered from a guilty conscience and from sickness which the guilty conscience brings. The devil will try to come again and sow sickness in the spirit and body of those who still live with a guilty conscience, who disregard the price which Jesus has already paid for their sins. These people are like someone who has been given an expensive gift but has not received it nor taken it home. If we have confessed our sins, we can free ourselves from a guilty conscience by remembering the price Jesus paid for our sins and then live boldly with the conviction that we have been forgiven.

We must also forgive the faults of our neighbors and others. Jesus said to Peter that he should forgive his neighbor as many as seventy times seven. Jesus gave us an example when He forgave a woman taken in adultery. Finally, He crowned His forgiving work by forgiving those who crucified Him as well as the thief who was crucified with Him.

We should forgive our neighbors in the name of Jesus Christ at any cost to ourselves. Our first duty is to obey the commandment of God then to form a warm relationship with those whom we forgive. The first condition on which God answers our prayers is that we forgive the offenses of others. Our forgiveness of others is also the condition on which God forgives us (Matt. 6:14-15).

It is by no means easy to forgive the faults of others, but since we have been forgiven by God and others, we also have the duty and responsibility to forgive others. No matter how difficult it may be, this must be done in our thinking, words and action. Otherwise God will not forgive us. For this task we must ask for help from the Holy Spirit.

Today many people have run into a blind alley where they cannot forgive others. Wives are in agony over the unfaithfulness of their husbands, and husbands are tormented because of the unfaithfulness of their wives. Other people are in sorrow and pain for the disobedience of their children and problems with family or neighbors. Through forgiveness, we destroy the fortress of the devil and build the kingdom of God. Forgiveness is so hard because the devil puts forth all his efforts to keep the memory of the pain there, lest we should forgive each other. But there is always great help available from the Holy Spirit, and that help is sufficient for every such need.

Miss Corrie ten Boom was a famous Dutch evangelist who was known worldwide. During World War II Miss ten Boom and her sister were sent to a Nazi concentration camp on the charge that they hid the Jews. Brutal torture at the concentration camps took the life of her sister. In spite of severe torture, however, Miss ten Boom escaped death. After returning to her homeland, she received a theological education and dedicated the rest of her life to ministering the gospel of the Lord Jesus Christ.

In the meantime she heard the voice of the Holy Spirit telling her to go to Germany and preach to the German people who were writhing in oppression from the defeat and guilt caused by their past, during which so many people were massacred.

Germany was indeed the last place she wanted to go, but since she wanted to obey the command of the Lord she went reluctantly and preached the gospel to the Germans. As they heard the gospel of forgiveness they rejoiced and many gave their lives to God. A great number of people were also set free from their sicknesses through her preaching.

One night when Corrie ten Boom had finished preaching and descended from the rostrum, a long line of people came forward to shake hands with her. Out of the crowd a man walked up and stretched out his hand. Suddenly it seemed as if her heart stopped. The man was none other than the soldier in the Nazi concentration camp who had commanded her to strip naked. Now the man was stretching out his hand to Corrie. But her arm seemed to be frozen, and she couldn't move. She couldn't shake hands with him. It was only a few seconds that he stood before her, but it seemed as if decades passed while her memory raced like a haunted thing to the former days. Though she had boldly preached the forgiveness of Christ that night, now she felt that she could by no means forgive this man who had mercilessly trampled her and her sister in her youth. In her heart Corrie ten Boom prayed, "Lord, I cannot possibly forgive this man. Help me to get out of this difficulty."

Then she heard the voice of the Holy Spirit again: "You know that I forgave those who killed Me, don't you? Can't you just shake hands with him?"

Hearing the voice of the Holy Spirit, she stretched out her hand which

150

seemed heavy as lead and shook hands with him. Then the love of Christ poured down from heaven. Engulfed by that love, she wept and forgave the soldier from her heart. She felt as if she became more than ten years younger as the healing spirit of Christ flowed in and over her and worked in her heart. Forgiveness is the only thing that brings us permanent healing.

In Europe there were countless people after World War II who became sick because they couldn't forgive the German people. Since the Germans were enemies whom they could not forget they hated them even in their dreams. To hate someone is one's choice, but one should never forget that hatred also eats away one's health. In order that the healing power of Jesus Christ may be manifested in our spirits and bodies, we must first receive forgiveness of sins and then live a life of forgiving others as we have been forgiven. This is God's supreme plan: "And all things are of God, who hath reconciled us to himself by Jesus Christ, and hath given to us the ministry of reconciliation; to wit that God was in Christ, reconciling the world unto himself, not imputing their trespasses unto them; and hath committed unto us the word of reconciliation" (2 Cor. 5:18,19).

Faith

The fourth condition necessary for healing is faith. The Bible reads: "Is any sick among you? let him call for the elders of the church; and let them pray over him, anointing him with oil in the name of the Lord: and the prayer of faith shall save the sick, and the Lord shall raise him up" (James 5:15).

The prayer of faith is neither a piece of good luck nor a windfall. It is a creative proclamation, seeing and expecting what is not now present as if it were already present. "Now faith is the substance of things hoped for, the evidence of things not seen" (Heb. 11:1).

Here the Greek word for substance is *hypostasis* which means title deed or government bond issued for the compensation of expropriated land. When we pray that our sickness may be healed, we should pray with conviction and faith as if we had the title deed in our hands. We should claim our health like the man who claims the ownership of land with a title deed. "But without faith it is impossible to please him: for he that cometh to God must believe that he is, and that he is a rewarder of them that diligently seek him" (Heb. 11:6). "But let him ask in faith, nothing wavering. For he that wavereth is like a wave of the sea driven with the wind and tossed. For let not that man think that he shall receive anything of the Lord. A doubleminded man is unstable in all his ways'' (James 1:6-8).

There are two kinds of faith. One is human faith, trusting to natural law and social institutions. It is based upon reason. Because we now have this kind of faith, we trust the band and deposit our money with it. We take a bus, trusting the driver. We also believe that today will be followed by tomorrow and winter will be followed by spring. This kind of faith is very natural and common to man. However, the faith in our hearts through the Holy Spirit is supernatural faith. It brings forth miracles. We can easily believe and accept the fact that the earth moves, but if it were not for the help of the Holy Spirit it would be difficult for people to believe the record of the Bible that Jesus is the Son of God and that we are saved by His atonement. We could not see the miracles of God either, except by such faith. Therefore, we should stand firmly on the Word. And we should welcome and accept the Holy Spirit as the One who creates faith in our hearts for salvation.

Is the faith which brings salvation different from the faith which experiences miracles? In the case of a man who is already saved, does he need some kind of special faith in order to experience signs and miracles? When we carefully read Jesus' words in Mark we clearly see that faith for salvation is identical with faith for signs and wonders: ''He that believeth and is baptized shall be saved; but he that believeth not shall be damned. And these signs shall follow them that believe'' (Mark 16:16-17).

In the above passage, the Greek words for the verb ''believe'' are *pisteusas* and *pisteusasi*, which are both derived from the same root. The former is the faith necessary for salvation and the latter necessary for seeing miracles. They are both the same faith. There is deep significance in the fact that our Lord combined salvation with the condition for experiencing miracles in the same faith. It is also suggested here that the grace of miracles and divine healing exists along with the grace of salvation in our own generation.

If signs and wonders, the gift of the working of miracles and the gift of healing, had existed only in the early church and are not manifested in today's church, the grace of salvation also should have ceased in the apostolic age. Likewise, if the grace of salvation of God continuously works in today's church, the work of miracles and healing should also happen in today's church as it did in the apostolic age.

Our Lord's last words, ''He that believeth and is baptized shall be saved;

but he that believeth not shall be damned,'' express His divine plan to continue working miracles as well as bringing salvation to His church until the end of this world (Mark 16:16-17).

Today, you are the people who accepted Jesus Christ as your Savior. Through this faith God saw you as righteous and sealed your salvation. When you recognize this fact and never doubt even a little bit, your sick body should also be healed. Prosperity should be your lot also. The faith that led you to salvation also leads you to signs and wonders.

Today, the chief weakness of many Christians is that they do not have a sure experience of personal encounter with Jesus as their Savior. Some people say they are Christians because they were born into a Christian family and were brought up in a Christian home. Others say that the encouragement of their relatives and friends bring them to the church. These people may be called ''Christians'' in some circles, but they have not yet become born-again believers. To be a born-again Christian one must have a personal experience with Jesus Christ. His family's experience cannot substitute for a personal relationship with Jesus Christ.

If one is not a Christian, in other words, if he is not born again so that Christ abides in him and he abides in Christ, that person is not yet in the grace of salvation. The faith of salvation has not been rooted in the heart, and consequently that one does not have faith for signs, wonders and miracles. Nevertheless, people who have the faith of salvation know well the power of their faith:

"Verily, verily, I say unto you, He that believeth on me, the works that I do shall he do also; and greater works than these shall he do; because I go unto my Father. And whatsoever ye shall ask in my name, that will I do'' (John 14:12-13). "If thou canst believe, all things are possible to him that believeth'' (Mark 9:23). "For verily I say unto you, That whosoever shall say unto this mountain, Be thou removed, and be thou cast into the sea; and shall not doubt in his heart, but shall believe that those things which he saith shall come to pass; he shall have whatsoever he saith'' (Mark 11:23).

Signs and wonders come to us through the faith we received at the time of salvation. Faith is not produced by human effort. Without an encounter with Jesus Christ no one can experience this faith. People who do not believe in signs and wonders and the working of miracles but only criticize have not had an encounter with Jesus Christ. They don't have the faith which comes from salvation even though they attend church. Faith born in the heart at the same time of salvation creates a fervent gratitude and deep love for the things of God. It also fills our hearts with expectation for the next world. When we think of God, who sent Jesus Christ to this world, we are compelled to thank Him for His great mercy and love because it included us.

The faith that believes in God's mercy also brings the miracle of healing to our sick bodies. God is the merciful Father who desired our health so much that He allowed His own Son to be whipped on our accord. Water and blood flowed from His broken body on the cross. God is the Father of love who heals and puts away the pain of sickness along with remission of sins. Our faith and gratitude for the mercy of God our Father brings healing to us.

In addition, we believe in the *authority* of the name of Jesus Christ. We find in the Bible that demons were cast out and the lame stood up at the proclamation of Jesus' name. Jesus' name brings miracles and healing as well as salvation: "Neither is there salvation in any other: for there is none other name under heaven given among men, whereby we must be saved" (Acts 4:12). "Then Peter said, Silver and gold have I none; but such as I have give I thee: In the name of Jesus Christ of Nazareth rise up and walk" (Acts 3:6).

In Jesus' name we can bind the devil and invoke the Spirit of healing. Jesus' name has the power to bring health and healing as well as salvation. There is compassion and kindness in the name of Jesus who bore our sickness.

In our minds we must draw a picture of ourselves as totally healed, on the authority of God's Word. Then the picture (the work of healing takes place) and faith will increase in our hearts. Also we should confess our healing with our mouth just as if we had regained our health already, because there is healing power in our speech. Since speech comes through thinking and faith in healing changes our thinking, our speech now commands the whole nervous system of the body so that it works to produce health. In accordance with that command, the energy of life is provided for the whole body.

More than anything else we must have faith. If we cannot receive faith by ordinary prayer, we must attend all-night prayer and fasting services so that we may have this faith in our hearts. We can't receive faith with mere intellectual understanding. Nor is faith a vague hope for the future. Faith is always a thing of the present. Now is the time you should fall in love with Jesus, and through that exciting relationship your faith will grow.

For this reason faith is known only to those who have it. When faith arises in our hearts, the Holy Spirit covers our hearts like a warm glow and increases our faith until He leads us to the signs and wonders.

When faith comes in, we have a changed image of ourselves which is a picture of our body in health and fully recovered from sickness. Like the woman who touched the hem of Jesus' garment, we should act on our faith. It is written in the Bible, ''If thou canst believe, all things are possible to him that believeth'' (Mark 9:23).

We must not go backwards after we have made a start in faith. Rather, we must put our faith into practice and move on to more new victories in Jesus.

Do Not Sin Again

''When the unclean spirit is gone out of a man, he walketh through dry places, seeking rest; and finding none, he saith, I will return unto my house whence I came out. And when he cometh, he findeth it swept and garnished. Then goeth he, and taketh to him seven other spirits more wicked than himself; and they enter in, and dwell there: and the last state of that man is worse than the first'' (Luke 11:24-26).

An unclean spirit can make people very sick. But when we believe that God is merciful and that Jesus bore our sicknesses, we can experience the miracle of deliverance and be healed. In this case, being healed means that the unclean spirit loosens his grip and lets us go free.

Man was originally to be a vessel or container. This vessel will contain either the Spirit of God or an unclean spirit. The vessel cannot remain empty. Unless we have invited Jesus into our lives after we are healed and made whole, the unclean spirit will try to take advantage and enter the cleansed vessel.

When I look back on the experience of my ministry, I believe the first year after sick people were healed was the most vulnerable period to them. During this period some of those people did not fill their lives with the Word of God, but worried and entertained thoughts like ''How terrible it would be if this disease recurred.'' Then the devil brought torment in his effort to kill, steal and destroy them through their fear.

When the unclean spirit has been cast out, we must be filled with the Holy Spirit, and from that day we should make our hearts become holy temples where God dwells. If we do this, the evil spirits cannot live in our hearts. In prayer, we should cast down imaginations and every high thing that exalts itself against the knowledge of God, and we must bring into captivity every thought to the obedience of Christ (2 Cor. 10:5).

We should continue to say, "I am crucified with Christ: nevertheless I live; yet not I, but Christ liveth in me: and the life which I now live in the flesh I live by the faith of the Son of God, who loved me, and gave himself for me" (Gal. 2:20).

5

A New Life

So far we have seen the inside of a wonderful house. We entered an entrance hall which was called "Our Good God." Then we saw the first room where we learned about the prosperity of our souls. Later, we saw the second room which led us further to the prosperity of all things we do, and lastly we see the third room in which we hear about the health of our body.

I suppose that you have already drawn a clear and beautiful picture in your heart of this house named Threefold Blessings. I believe you now earnestly desire to live in all the rooms of this house no matter what other people may do. Not only do you want to live in a house like this yourself, but you probably want to hand it down to your children and grandchildren also.

This house can be yours. So far I have not shown you someone else's house, but I have shown you a house which truly can be yours! If it were a house that we could not have, we wouldn't need to waste our time and energy examining it. This house is newly furnished inside and outside, waiting for its owner to come. You are welcome to put your name on the mail box and on the front door and to start living there right now.

How beautiful and blessed are those rooms which you have looked at so far! This is the house of blessing which will bring prosperity to your soul in all things, health to your body and the blessings of a more abundant life.. This house is for you.

If only you confess, "This house is mine," it will be registered in your name in heaven and on earth, and it will be proven so. We invite you to come now. Put your name on the mail box and on the front door and move in. After moving in, you must now adapt your life to the dignity of the house. You must start a new life by living in all the rooms of your new house. You must be careful to use all that was planned and furnished for your house, to meet every need until Jesus comes. If you do that, you will become master of your entire life both in name and reality.

We are now going to look into the conditions necessary for becoming the master of the house of Threefold Blessings. When you remember these and practice them diligently, you will live as master of your life in all respects.

Hang New Portraits

However good the house may be where we live, we cannot live without seeing the rain, wind and storms which come in successive seasons. Likewise, though we live a life of threefold blessings, we can't avoid trials and tribulations which come from time to time during the journey of our life. When unbelievers in the world are swept away by these, however, we who live in this house of threefold blessings do not waver nor fear. Why? Because we know that the circumstances around us are changing, not we ourselves. Since we have the ability to distinguish clearly subjectivity from objectivity, the happenings around us cannot sway us. We have become established in Christ. We have a new image of ourselves.

When trials and tribulations approach, we offer thanksgiving and praise that the salvation of God may be manifested in our living as we go through the trials (Ps. 50:23). Even if clouds or the power of darkness spreads over our lives, we can still sing a hymn and march on like Paul, Silas and the disciples (Matt. 26:30).

Those who have established themselves in Christ are full of confidence in every respect, and they have clothed their thinking and words with understanding, forbearance and love. They neither run out of patience, collapse in despair nor pridefully build up a "tower of Babel" (Gen. 11:1-9). They know for certain where they came from, why they are living and where they are going.

Let's take a look at a Christian's way of life after he has established himself in the Lord.

True Freedom

Those who have established themselves in the threefold blessings of Christ should live in true freedom. Taking a look around the house, the threefold blessings which we have seen and realized so far consist of the

158

truth in the Word of God. Our Lord said, "And ye shall know the truth, and the truth shall make you free" (John 8:32).

We have certainly seen and known that Jesus Christ set us free through His crucifixion. He bore all our sins, curses and sicknesses. "If the Son therefore shall make you free, ye shall be free indeed" (John 8:36).

Specifically, from what have we been set free? And from what should we be set free?

First, we have been set free from covetousness. "Mortify therefore your members which are upon the earth; fornication, uncleanness, inordinate affection, evil concupiscence, and covetousness, which is idolatry" (Col. 3:5).

Since covetousness is idolatry, and since God destroys idolaters, it is certain that we would have been killed unless we had been delivered from covetousness. Because of covetousness, numerous leaders have disappeared and innumerable businessmen have failed in their businesses. Not infrequently we see around us those families which are broken because of covetousness.

Today thousands of people are seeking God and receiving divine grace. Others are eager to meet Jesus, but because they do not give up their covetousness they are going away in sorrow like the rich young man mentioned in the Bible (Luke 18:23). Covetousness arises when man desires something that someone else has but which he cannot have. Covetousness is greed.

But the person who understands what the threefold blessings contain at once realizes how narrow-minded and shallow human greed and covetousness are. I presume by now you heartily admit that nothing is better than the blessings which are in this house!

Those who have received the threefold blessings have already given up covetousness. Such a person can deeply understand what Jesus said: "But seek ye first the kingdom of God, and his righteousness; and all these things shall be added unto you" (Matt. 6:33).

People who have been cleansed from covetousness know the secret of salvation and blessing through the power of Jesus Christ.

Second, those who have been established in the threefold blessings are set free from the returning habit of sin. The Bible says, "There is none righteous, no, not one" (Rom. 3:10) and "All have sinned, and come short of the glory of God" (Rom. 3:23).

Though the power of sin has been broken and we have been set free from a guilty conscience, the temptation of those habits will allure us from time to time. This is because the habit still remains in us until it is completely uprooted. Even the apostle Paul deplored this fact: "So then with the mind I myself serve the law of God; but with the flesh the law of sin" (Rom. 7:25).

Since we are still in the flesh, sometimes we may stumble because of weakness. There are other times when we may commit sin in spite of knowing that we are doing wrong. For this reason the Holy Spirit groans within us (Rom. 8:26). He also restrains our every move if we do sin, in an effort to bring us back to repentance. If we allow Him to speak to us, He will lead us back to Jesus for repentance and cleansing.

However if we willfully repeat the same sin again and again and persist in going our own way, He will eventually remove His presence from our lives and it will be easy for us to fall into bondage again. This is how Christians sometimes fall into bondage. Habitual sin is usually committed because one does not feel remorse for sin. The man who has already entered the threefold blessings of Christ has experienced a quickening in his spirit and is communicating with God. If a sin is developing into a habit, he will not be able to bear it because of the pangs of his conscience. God also gives him a trial that brings him back. But he who lives in the house of threefold blessings can be free from habits of sin. These blessings enable him to live above habitual sin.

Third, we are set free from uneasiness and fears. The Bible warns us, "In the last days perilous times shall come" (2 Tim. 3:1).

As foretold in God's Word, innumerable troubles are approaching our world—spiritual nihilism, the exhaustion of natural resources, unemployment, poverty, disease, wars and rumors of wars. On account of these, some people are living in constant uneasiness, care, anxiety and impatience. Who can escape this uneasiness and fear?

Nobody can become free except those who have entered the threefold blessings. We believe in a good God. God within us is a good God who desires that we may prosper and be in health, even as our soul prospers. Whatever happens to us, we accept those things with joy. Happy situations are in themselves good, and unpleasant situations will turn out to be good. However fierce the storms and tempests may rage in our everyday living, we will not be unsettled but we will grip firmly the Word of God which encourages us: "We know that all things work together for good to them that love God, to them who are the called according to his purpose" (Rom. 8:28). We declare boldly: "Who shall separate us from the love of Christ? shall tribulation, or distress, or persecution, or famine, or nakedness, or peril, or sword?'' (Rom. 8:35).

Gehazi trembled in fear as he saw a swarming host of the Syrian army. But when his spiritual eyes were opened, he could boldly confess, "They that be with us are more than be with them" (2 Kings 6:16). We who believe that God created heaven and earth and all things in them can be set free from all kinds of uneasiness and fears of life: "For we walk by faith, not by sight" (2 Cor. 5:7).

Fourth, we are set free from death. As long as we live in this world, the shadow of death hangs around us, not leaving for a moment. At any time and place where we are living, we can be oppressed by the fear of death. However healthy, learned, virtuous or rich a man may be, once death approaches and knocks at his door, he must remove his hands from whatever he has been doing. Who can make us avoid such death?

Throughout history a countless number of great wise men and saints came and went but no one ever returned. No one has been able to tell us what is beyond death. People are afraid of the unknown world which lies beyond death, not of the moment of death.

When Jesus Christ came to this earth, however, He showed us what is beyond death. By His crucifixion and resurrection on the third day, He showed us there is resurrection beyond death. He also showed us that those who commit sin will be cast into the lake of unquenchable fire and brimstone, but those who are sanctified through faith in Jesus Christ will live in glory and splendor with the host of angels, praising God in heaven forever. And He said to us, "I am the resurrection, and the life: he that believeth in me, though he were dead, yet shall he live: and whosoever liveth and believeth in me shall never die. Believest thou this?" (John 11:25,26). "Let not your heart be troubled: ye believe in God, believe also in me. In my Father's house are many mansions" (John 14:1,2).

The apostle Paul said with faith, "For we know that if our earthly house of this tabernacle were dissolved, we have a building of God, an house not made with hands, eternal in the heavens" (2 Cor. 5:1).

Again, for this reason, we who dwell in the grace of the threefold blessings are entitled to freedom from death. The new house we live in is wonderful, but how much more wonderful will that kingdom be for which God is preparing us! With deep joy and anticipation in our hearts, we say loudly, "Amen. Even so, come, Lord Jesus" (Rev. 22:20).

We who have experienced the threefold blessings have become free from covetousness, habits of sin, uneasiness, fear of life and fear of death. We can live free from worldly cares. By believing in Jesus Christ, welcoming and accepting Him, we can receive at once this great peace which the Tao and all other religious systems tried to obtain but never did achieve. Confess with your mouth that you are already free. Nothing but real freedom can lead you to God-given success from now till eternity. "Now the Lord is that Spirit: and where the Spirit of the Lord is, there is liberty" (2 Cor. 3:17).

That Which Is Everlasting

What should the people be like who live in the house of threefold blessings, who have put their name on the deed and on the mail box and the door? How is their daily living different from that of other people? In order that we may live successfully every day, we should continually have the following experiences.

First, we should have a forgiving and loving spirit. Forgiveness and love are both necessary for our own experience with God and right relations with our neighbors. If we have not been forgiven by God we cannot call God our Father. Because we have been forgiven, we must forgive others also.

If Jesus had not so loved the world, He would not have come to this earth for us. In order that we may continually live in the threefold blessings, we must have a continual spirit of forgiveness and love, as Jesus had. When we fail to forgive and love others, we must pray for the help of the Holy Spirit and He will enable us to forgive and love. "Though I speak with the tongues of men and of angels, and have not charity, I am become as sounding brass, or a tinkling cymbal. And though I have the gift of prophecy, and understand all mysteries, and all knowledge; and though I have all faith, so that I could remove mountains, and have not charity, I am nothing. And though I bestow all my goods to feed the poor, and though I give my body to be burned, and have not charity, it profiteth me nothing" (1 Cor. 13:1-3).

Love is a flame of life which vitalizes our being. However physically comfortable our homes may be, without love they are like deserted houses with nothing but cold air. Those who receive the threefold blessings of Christ and live in them should persist in showing forgiveness and love in their lives every day.

Second, we should always have faith. If we lose faith, all of our human and social relationships will collapse from that moment. We must believe God means what He says.

If our faith in God cools, our relationship with Him will cool also. If we want to live forever in the house of threefold blessings, we must always be watchful in prayer lest our faith in our good God should fade.

Faith also brings forth hope. Unless we believe that God will give us all good things, we cannot have hope either. However, if we believe that God is our good Father, we should also strongly desire and believe that God will reward His children with the good things they ask for.

In addition, we should also have eternal hope, not just hope for living in this world, but for our life in the coming world: "If in this life only we have hope in Christ, we are of all men most miserable" (1 Cor. 15:19).

"Blessed be the God and Father of our Lord Jesus Christ, which according to his abundant mercy hath begotten us again into a living hope by the resurrection of Jesus Christ from the dead, to an inheritance incorruptible, and undefiled, and that fadeth not away, reserved in heaven for you" (1 Pet. 1:3-4).

Forgiveness, love, faith and hope—these are the characteristics of the life which is replete with the threefold blessings of Christ.

The Man in the Mirror

Not a day passes that we do not look in the mirror. The purpose of looking in the mirror is not merely to keep ourselves neat and trim, but to find the identity between the person reflected in the mirror and the person who is looking at that image of himself. I can only be satisfied when the person reflected in the mirror is identical with the person pictured in my heart.

This is also true in the lives of Christians. We can lead an enthusiastic and joyful Christian life only when there is identity between the born-again person (the one reflected in the mirror) and the true person in ordinary life (the one looking into the mirror). When there is no identity between these two, the person in the mirror is only a person who has crossed over the threshold of a church to attend a service and walked out to return home the same way he was before.

When we were the children of darkness, it mattered very little who we were. At that time our thoughts and actions were neither moral nor spiritual, because we were the children of the devil. However, if we confess that Jesus Christ is our Lord and Savior, believing in the power of His blood, we should daily look into the spiritual mirror, the Word of God, and allow the Holy Spirit to reveal us to ourselves: "But we all, with open face beholding as in a glass the glory of the Lord, are changed into the same image from glory to glory even as by the Spirit of the Lord" (2 Cor. 3:18).

After we have been changed into His image, where and how can we see the glory of the Lord in our lives? The Bible says, "But of him are ye in Christ Jesus, who of God is made unto us wisdom, and righteousness, and sanctification, and redemption" (1 Cor. 1:30). "Therefore if any man be in Christ, he is a new creature: old things are passed away; behold, all things are become new" (2 Cor. 5:17).

I cannot find the glory of Christ in my "old man," but I can find that glory in the new person I am in Christ Jesus, the one which was transformed by the death and resurrection of Christ. In the new image, which was cleansed of a guilty conscience, delivered from the oppression of the devil and set free from the curse, sickness and death, we see the glorious image of Christ. Through His redemption at the cross we see a whole new and different world that has been established by Jesus Christ. When we daily look at this new inner man, daily identifying ourselves with him, we can for the first time have the image of Christ. This is the very image of God, created in the likeness of His own nature and plan.

As human beings, we must go out into the world every day to perform our jobs. We cannot live one day without hearing sinful language and seeing evil all around us. Unless our image is renewed every day and every moment, we will lose our identity and go astray.

How can we renew our image continuously? Should we prepare our portrait or statue and look at it every day? No, we don't need to do that. Through the Word of God and prayer we renew our minds daily and draw a fresh new image of who we are in Christ. Our lives are thus transformed again and again.

So far we have drawn a picture of a Christian who is not only established in the threefold blessings but who has been transformed and matured. Whoever receives Christ and lives in the threefold blessings is also established in the Lord.

"Loose Him and Let Him Go"

The grave where Lazarus was buried was silent. Just outside the tomb Mary and Martha wept bitterly, and the people murmured, saying, "Behold how he loved him!...Could not this man, which opened the eyes of the blind, have caused that even this man should not have died?" (John 11:36-37). Jesus, who was observing this scene, opened His mouth and gave a creative command with a loud voice, "Lazarus, come forth" (John 11:43).

According to Jesus' words, Lazarus rose and came out, but because his hands and feet were bound by grave clothes, fold on fold, he could not walk or speak. If Lazarus had remained in that bound state, it would have been much the same as if he were dead. Jesus said again, however, "Loose him and let him go." This command of our Lord is a good word for us today. Jesus called and quickened us who had been dead in sin. He opened our eyes to the threefold blessings and gave us hope for His eternal kingdom. But knowledge avails little unless it is put into practice. You should make the most of it so that it may become a blessing to you. If you just pass by the threefold blessings, knowing them by name but not living in them, they can't change your life a bit.

You should not only recognize that these blessings are for you, but also loose the power of the threefold blessings and live in them! When you welcome and receive the Holy Spirit, He will transform you so that you can live in them. You should ask Jesus Christ to seal your thoughts, words and actions with the threefold blessings and then let them work in your life.

Confess the threefold blessings with your mouth! Say now that it has become well with your soul! Testify this boldly to your neighbors! This is how to loose the power of the threefold blessings so that your soul may truly prosper. Now confess that you have prospered in all things. Behave as one who has succeeded, and you will loose the power of prosperity in your daily living. Confess with your mouth and believe that you have been made whole, and the Holy Spirit will unleash the healing that makes you whole.

Behold your changed image! Listen to your changed words! You are now full of the threefold blessings of Christ. Wherever you go, blessings are poured out upon you. Wherever you go, vitality overflows. You are now a great victor through the Word of God!

OTHER PUBLICATIONS
OF INTEREST FROM
CREATION HOUSE

The Emerging Christian Woman
by Anne Gimenez

Women are on the move. They are shaking off many years of silence and passivity. Inspired by the Spirit, they are assuming their proper roles of leadership in the body of Christ. Anne believes Christ is calling Christian women to take a lead in bringing new life, healing and unity to the church. $4.95

Spiritual Power and Church Growth
by C. Peter Wagner

Why do some churches grow like wildfire? How can we learn from this marvelously successful church growth movement? C. Peter Wagner identifies the main reasons for the expansion of Pentecostal churches and articulates key principles behind their growth in Latin America. With examples, stories and facts, he writes about how to engage the power of the Holy Spirit; involving new Christians in ministry; cell groups; training leaders in service; the importance of signs and wonders; and other valuable principles. $6.95

OTHER PUBLICATIONS
OF INTEREST FROM
CREATION HOUSE

Could You Not Tarry One Hour?
by Larry Lea

To many Christians prayer is a drudgery. Larry Lea has discovered that prayer can be a pleasure and we can learn how to enjoy it. The more we learn to "tarry one hour," the more we will grow in likeness to Christ and the more we will be able to bring His timeless message to a world in pain. $12.95

ISBN 0-88419-198-2   Hardback

Riding the Wind
Your Life in the Holy Spirit
by Everett (Terry) L. Fullam

Raise your sails and let the gentle breezes of the Holy Spirit move in your life. Learn more about Him and His availability to you in this personal and biblical book by one of America's finest teachers. $7.95

ISBN 0-88419-196-6   Trade Paper

Available at your Christian bookstore or from:

Creation House
190 N. Westmonte Drive
Altamonte Springs, FL 32714
(305) 869-5005

Charisma—the magazine about Spirit-led living—offers dynamic teaching and insight for charismatic believers who want to grow and stay informed. *Charisma* helps you keep up-to-date on current events and happenings throughout the body of Christ. You will come to respect *Charisma*'s honest, objective reporting on the controversial issues shaping our contemporary society. *Charisma* also brings you delightful and helpful interviews with many of the top Christian teachers, evangelists, authors, preachers and personalities.

You'll appreciate *Charisma*'s columnists such as Marilyn Hickey, Larry Lea and Jamie Buckingham. They share with you fresh insights to the Word of God. To subscribe to *Charisma* today send just $16.97 to: *Charisma,* Box 861, Farmingdale, NY 11737, or call toll-free (with your credit card handy) 1-800-227-5782. You'll receive a full year (12 issues) of some of the most interesting Christian reading available. Your first issue should arrive in about six to eight weeks from the time you subscribe. Subscribe today—you don't want to miss an issue.

Ministries Today

Ministries Today is a practical bi-monthly journal for church leaders. Whether you're a pastor, music leader, deacon, youth minister or active lay leader you'll find every issue offers you practical helps and advice on administrative, pastoral and educational issues. *Ministries Today*'s articles carefully blend proven leadership techniques with spiritual sensitivity.

Ministries Today will help you meet the challenges of contemporary church leadership in a stress-filled world. You will gain insights from resources and specialists in the areas of counseling, communications and administration—financial advisors, builders, tax experts, medical and legal professionals and others with specific expertise in church-related matters.

Ministries Today is right on target, addressing tough topics and providing practical and proven leadership insights with each issue.

Become a well-informed leader and subscribe now to *Ministries Today*. Send just $18 to: *Ministries Today*, P.O. Box 881, Farmingdale, NY 11737. You'll receive a full year (six issues) of practical, sensible insight and advice. Order today.

NOTES

NOTES

NOTES

NOTES